STRATFORD PAPERS

ON *Shakespeare*

*delivered at the 1961
Shakespeare Seminar
sponsored by the Universities
of Canada in co-operation
with the Stratford Festival
Theatre through the offices
of the Department of
Extension of McMaster
University*

W. J. GAGE LIMITED, TORONTO

Designed by Arnold Rockman, MTDC

Printed and bound in Canada, 1962

Contents

v

B. W. JACKSON

Introduction

Over the years Shakespeare has provided pleasure and entertainment for millions; for many of us he has provided a part or all of our livelihood as well. I suppose that in all history he has been the world's largest single employer of highly skilled labour: theatre people, scholars, teachers, critics and miscellaneous writers, painters, musicians, architects, publishers and ticket-agents. The Shakespeare Industry has never been more prosperous than in our time. It is not without point to consider that, if he were to suffer an eclipse, if the millions were suddenly to reject him, an impressive number of us would be hard put to it to find a substitute on which to exercise our talents and ingenuity.

> The cease of majesty
> Dies not alone . . . it is a massy wheel,
> Fix'd on the summit of the highest mount,
> To whose huge spokes ten thousand lesser things
> Are mortis'd and adjoin'd; which, when it falls
> Each small annexment, petty consequence
> Attends the boisterous ruin.

Fortunately there seems to be little danger that Shakespeare will fall from eminence, but it is not unrealistic to suggest that the 'highest mount' on which he sits is composed not only of scholarly, critical and theatrical approval, but also in considerable part of public favour. Those in the Industry have helped to create this public favour—this is particularly true of those in the theatre—but essentially it depends on Shakespeare's own excellence, and on a public that has been able to recognize it.

The first factor will remain constant; it seems likely that the second will too, since it has already for centuries survived the aberrations of some scholars, teachers, critics, directors and actors. This is not, then, an awful warning to the professionals that they must serve the public or perish, but it may serve to remind some of us that Shakespeare is public property, and that the Shakespeare Industry is in a sense, therefore, a public utility upon whose employees there rests some obligation to consider the public interest.

In the theatre, where the obligation has been most obvious and where attention to it has been most remunerative, it has been most completely and most faithfully fulfilled. Yet even here there is sometimes a tendency to look on the public as a necessary nuisance, and to produce the plays in defiance not only of the texts but also of the audience. Actors, in their worst moments, will make a mystery of their craft, and speak as if only they know what Shakespeare is all about. And yet there have been many mediocre or bad productions of his plays. On the other hand, I have never seen a good production that has not held its audience, except for a few scholars and critics whose grumblings give notice that they are forever impervious to pleasure.

The obligation upon scholars is not so obvious; the

concentration upon books that their work demands, and
the relative isolation that is one of its conditions can be
expected to reduce their awareness of the audience so
that, when they think of it at all, as they do when they
produce their own books and papers, they think of it
as made up of other scholars: that is, of those who can
understand what they are talking about.

The hungry sheep look up and are not fed.

The professional critic of the plays, whether as theatre
or literature, speaks as directly to the public as does the
actor. If it is anyone's business to clarify, to illuminate,
to provide a catalyst for enjoyment, one might assume
that this is the obligation of the critic. Yet many of the
tribe seem to believe that confusion and darkness best
become their pronouncements on the plays as literature,
or that it is their duty to warn the public that they are
being grossly taken in if they find themselves giving
way to any sensations of pleasure or delight while at
the theatre.

Finally, there is internecine bickering within the
Industry. Directors and actors, the excellence of whose
productions has depended in no inconsiderable part on
the painstaking work of generations of scholars, will
speak as if scholarship is at best a parasitic growth on
the body of the plays, and at worst a malignant disease
from the ravages of which the theatre is forever hard
pressed to save Shakespeare's works. On the other hand,
sound and eminent scholars, fresh from an enchanting
performance of a play, have been heard rumbling with
indignation, their evening ruined by one or two minor
discrepancies in the text, or by a few bits of business
that did not square with their notion of the play.

Critics are unloved; scholars speak of them as if they were intellectually impoverished relatives, and the actors, who "never read their columns," are outraged by the opinions expressed there. Yet the opinions are frequently reasonable, and the director who has launched an Eskimo *Lear* may be restrained from rushing too precipitously into a Ubangi *Tempest* or a Mau Mau *Titus Andronicus* by the strictures of a temperate critic. Meanwhile the critics will have their revenge for indignities heaped upon them by sniping at the players, and by remaining resolutely out of touch with the last fifty years of scholarship.

The three groups, players, scholars and critics, agree only in this: that the fourth group, the teachers, profane the plays by using them as weapons to make their charges 'hate Shakespeare forever,' thereby presumably restricting Shakespeare's audience in each generation to those who have never been to school. In truth, it is the teachers who do more than any others to bring Shakespeare to the hearts and minds of the multitude, and although it may be a deplorable fact that the teacher cannot enlighten his students with a full-dress professional production of each play he takes up with them, it seems ungracious to charge him with malfeasance on that account. The schoolboy who tells you he hates Shakespeare will usually tell you that he hates all poetry and a good many other studies as well. Only an astonishing naiveté about school and schoolboys will take his statement seriously, or blame his teacher for it. As for those adults who tell you bitterly that they got nothing out of Shakespeare at school, it seems as likely an assumption that they themselves have experienced

a late flowering of sensibility as that an inept teacher
could nevertheless have been so influential as totally to
obliterate for them those beauties which they now pro-
fess to find in the plays. For there is this about teachers:
most of them go at their job with a decent humility
about Shakespeare and toward their students. I have
never heard a teacher cherishing the absurd notion that
he owned Shakespeare.

All this is exaggerated, but I hope there is enough
truth in it to explain why the layman who cares for
Shakespeare—and that layman's name is legion—is often
puzzled by what he takes to be the attitudes of the
people in the Industry. And there are times when he
feels shut out, when his modesty allows him the impression that there must be mysteries about the plays which
are beyond his capabilities. There is an irony in this,
since it may be suspected that, if the pleasure that the
professional derives from the plays differs in kind from
that derived by the enthusiastic and intelligent layman,
it is the professional who is the loser.

Be that as it may, the Seminars on Shakespeare, begun at Stratford, Ontario, in the summer of 1960, continued in 1961, and planned again for 1962, are an
attempt to provide a meeting place for professionals
and laymen where they can see each other at short
range, exchange enthusiasms when they see eye to eye,
and have at it with a will when they disagree.

At such meetings it is a handful of professionals who
take the lead. And here, in spite of what has been said
above, it is gladly admitted that the scholars, players and
critics taking part in these Seminars as speakers or leaders of discussion have been generous, lucid and helpful

beyond any obligation which even the trusteeship of a public utility might impose upon them; indeed, to such a degree that one would be forced to suggest that contact with the layman brings out the best in them if one did not already know that these particular people were exceptions anyway to the types described above. Or perhaps it is more accurate to say that the 'types' themselves are the exceptions, and that most of those within the Shakespeare Industry can be counted upon to give generously of their time and talents for the benefit of the layman whenever they get the chance. Certainly the chance offered by the Seminars has made this apparent.

The Seminars are planned to serve those members of Shakespeare's wide public who, coming to Stratford to see the plays, may have the time and the inclination to add to their programme of play-going the opportunity to hear some lectures, take part in some formal discussions, and derive whatever pleasures and benefits they may from each other's society not only at these functions but at meals and elsewhere. Such a group is certain to be heterogeneous; an interest in Shakespeare is the only thing one can be sure they will have in common. Yet it is enough; in the past two summers it has proven sufficient to draw together the scholar and the student, the professional and the layman, in agreeable company.

And the purpose of these publications, which follow the Seminars and contain the talks and lectures delivered at them, is in so far as it is possible an extension of the purpose of the Seminars themselves. It is felt that the relatively small group who hear the lectures during the summer must be only a microcosmic representation of a larger number who will enjoy the lectures if they are made available.

So that, although scholars of eminence have contributed to this collection of papers and to its predecessor, these volumes are not learned journals; they are not addressed primarily to scholars, their main interest is not in detailed scholarly research, and they are not concerned in the first place with uttering new critical points of view. There are already numerous excellent journals devoted to these excellent purposes.

This is not to say that scholars should find nothing to interest them in these pages, that the results of detailed research are not evident, nor that the critical viewpoints expressed have necessarily been heard before. I am talking here about the purpose for which these lectures were prepared and delivered, and not about what any one or more of them may achieve beyond that purpose. And that purpose is, of course, to make available to the layman, for his better understanding and fuller enjoyment of Shakespeare, some of the things that the professionals know, as well as the attitudes and perceptions they have achieved during lifetimes devoted to his works. However, the book is not entirely given over to the professionals; among the authors there are some who modestly claim to be laymen. And this is of all the more interest because it reminds us that the Seminars themselves do provide an opportunity for a two-way exchange of opinion.

If the volume is not intended as a learned journal, it may be supposed that it is meant to have 'popular' appeal, but the word 'popular,' along with its idiotic offspring 'popularize,' is in such disrepute that it would be unjust to apply it to the purpose of this publication. And yet, if it be conceded that Shakespeare is popular in our time, I suppose that it is the right word. For these papers were intended in the first place for those who have an interest in Shakespeare that is not vested, by vocation or circumstance, in scholarship or criticism or stage production. I say 'in the first place' because one cannot draw hard and fast lines here; the papers should be of some interest to anyone who finds himself in Shakespeare's audience. Yet the great majority of that audience is made up of people who have no professional interest in his works, or of people, teachers for instance, whose professional interest touches his works now and again, but who cannot afford to devote a lifetime to their study. It is significant, if obvious, that there is no way to speak of this large group in the mass except as Shakespeare's audience, for the individual members represent, I suppose, almost every vocation of man.

Speaking recently to a conference of scholars, the Director of the Folger Shakespeare Library said:

> We do not need to belabour the point that Shakespeare is of enormous interest to the peoples of every continent. But perhaps it might be profitable for us to contemplate for a few moments the problems, the responsibilities, and the obligations that this vast interest imposes upon us, an accredited body of scholars, whose presumed duty it is to make Shakespeare better understood and appreciated by the multitude who read him or see his plays acted on the stage.

And about his own library, he remarked:

> Some of our clients are professional scholars like yourselves; some are teachers; some are students;

a surprising number can be classified as the general
public. They are concerned with Shakespeare and
his meaning on various levels of understanding.
And they all ask questions that we find hard to
answer.[1]

The Seminars are an attempt to do something about
the obligation that Dr. Wright mentions. So, too, is
the publication of these volumes.

To the professionals, to the scholars, the players and
the critics, the layman owes an enormous debt for the
pleasure he derives from Shakespeare. That is recognized. But it is often not recognized that scholar and
player and critic owe a debt to the layman. In their
worst moments, they speak as if the layman's interest
in the plays was of their creation. That they had a hand
in the matter is obvious, but to claim all the credit
neglects the part that Shakespeare himself has played.
And if it is agreed that credit should go to him for
writing the plays, it should be equally clear that credit
should go to the lay audience that can receive the plays
with such enthusiasm. The roles of the professionals
are important, but they are important largely because
they are intermediary. Shakespeare without an audience
would be a different master for each of them.

To the persons who have contributed their papers to
this book our debt is obvious, and I can do no more
than note it inadequately here, but there are others,
whose names do not appear in the following pages,
whose kindness, talents and generosity had much to
do with the success of the Seminars. We owe a special

1. Louis B. Wright, "An Obligation to Shakespeare and the Public," a talk
given at the International Shakespeare Conference at Stratford-upon-Avon,
August 28, 1961.

debt of gratitude to Mr. Sidney Fisher of Montreal for his permission to use books from his valuable collection during our sessions. To Professor Francis Fergusson of Rutgers University, Mr. Herbert Whittaker of the *Globe and Mail,* Mr. Arnold Edinborough of *Saturday Night,* Mr. George McCowan and Mr. Douglas Campbell of the Festival Theatre, and to Professor David Galloway of the University of New Brunswick, all of whom led discussion groups, we owe the enormous gratitude that any enterprise must feel for its unsung heroes. Our thanks are again due, and willingly paid, to the people of the Festival Theatre, Mr. Victor Polley, Mr. Bruce Swerdfager, Mr. Bruce McDonald, Mrs. Catherine Roeder, Mr. Jack Karr, Mr. Norman Freeman, who not only make things possible but also pleasant for us. And here a special thanks must be offered to Mr. Paul Scofield and to his wife, Miss Joy Parker, for their handsome gift of a poetry reading during the Second Seminar. And, finally, our thanks to the actors and actresses of the Festival Theatre who made possible those most enjoyable of events, the Actors' Symposiums: Miss Helen Burns, Miss Zoe Caldwell, Miss Amelia Hall, Mr. Eric Christmas, Mr. John Colicos, Mr. Peter Donat, Mr. Max Helpmann, and Mr. Leon Major.

I must, in closing, express my own gratitude to the members of the Operating Committee: Professor M. A. King of the Ontario Agricultural College, and Professor William McCallion and Mr. Peter Smith of the Department of Extension of McMaster University. To each of these men all those who attended the Seminars are much indebted, but to Mr. Smith in particular who, as Secretary, is the most hard pressed, a special reward is

due, but perhaps not paid by simply allowing him to
write the biographical notes for this volume.

                                                    BWJ.

McMaster University,
March 14, 1962.

Northrop Frye, the principal lecturer in the first seminar, is a graduate of the University of Toronto and Merton College, Oxford. The whole of his teaching, apart from visiting terms at six North American universities, has been done at Victoria College in the University of Toronto of which he is now the Principal as well as Professor of English. His major publications are *Fearful Symmetry,* a study of William Blake, and *Anatomy of Criticism,* but in addition he has contributed chapters or essays to several books, and has edited many others including the Modern Library edition of Blake, the Rinehart edition of Milton, and *The Tempest* in the Pelican Shakespeare. Since 1951 he has been a member of the Royal Society of Canada, from which he received, in 1958, the Lorne Pierce Medal for distinguished contributions to Canadian literature; he is, too, a member of the Executive Council of the Modern Languages Association of America.

NORTHROP FRYE

Shakespeare's

experimental comedy

When Elizabethan drama first developed, comedy was far better supplied than tragedy was with models, precedents, and ready-made characters and themes. It had about two dozen of the adaptations from Greek New Comedy made by Plautus and Terence. Shakespeare's early *Comedy of Errors* is based on Plautus's *Menaechmi,* with subsidiary themes from other plays of Plautus. It also has some romance themes used later in *Pericles,* and a range of imagery and emotion far beyond anything that Plautus ever knew existed, but still it goes down in the handbooks as an adaptation of Plautus. The influence of the Romans was expanded and reinforced by a Renaissance Italian influence, clearly marked in *The Two Gentlemen of Verona* and *The Taming of the Shrew,* and which included the popular drama of the *commedia dell'arte.* This latter, with its stock characters and half-improvised plots, continued to fascinate Shakespeare up to *The Tempest.* The stock characters introduced into *Love's Labour's Lost* are types that run through the whole history of comedy. Five of them are summarized by Berowne as "The pedant, the braggart, the hedge-priest, the fool, and the boy." In the "hedge-priest" Nathaniel, who spends a scene flattering Holofernes and is finally rewarded with an invitation to dinner, we recognize a mutation of the Classical parasite. To these Shakespeare adds the rural constable, who, as you will be reminded by *The Pirates of Penzance,* has remained a comic figure ever since.

Shakespeare's immediate predecessors, Peele, Greene, and more especially Lyly, had already transformed a comedy of situation into a comedy of wit and dialogue. We have comedy of situation, in a fairly literal sense, in the early *Gammer Gurton's Needle,* where after a great deal of running around trying to find a lost needle, a clown named Hodge sits down suddenly, jumps up with a yell, and announces that he now knows where the needle is. The change from this to the delicate fairy-tale fantasies of Peele and Lyly had taken place before Shakespeare had well started. Perhaps the attention paid to Moth, who is encouraged with a zeal worthy of a modern progressive school, reflects the popularity of the children's companies for whom Lyly wrote.

The admixture of masque in *Love's Labour's Lost* is another influence making for courtly refinement. There is one masque in particular that I have occasionally wondered about in connection with *Love's Labour's Lost.* It is a brilliant little sketch of Sir Philip Sidney's, not published till 1598 but of course written much earlier, and called by Sidney's editor *The Lady of May.* It introduces a pedantic schoolmaster who talks quite like Holofernes, including an overuse of alliteration, and another speaker who complains that the young shepherds' mistresses have too much wit, which makes "loving labours" folly and causes the lovers to bewail their "lost labour."

Love's Labour's Lost is the only play of Shakespeare which suggests that the original audience may have been enjoying a good deal that we cannot now recapture. The sense that some of the characters are take-offs on contemporary personalities is strong, and several models have been proposed, including Florio, Gabriel Harvey, and others. About thirty years ago it was suggested that the play was a satire on an alleged "school of night," involving Chapman and Raleigh, but this suggestion has not been developed very far. Some passages in the dialogue remain mysterious to me: when Holofornes, for instance, says: "Sir, tell me not of the father: I do fear colourable colours," "colourable colours" meaning apparently "plausible excuses," I have not the faintest notion what he means. Nor do I know what significance, if any, is to be attached to the fact that the king's associates bear names of leaders in the French religious wars.

Love's Labour's Lost has all the marks of a highly sophisticated play, and a play that must have been physically close to a sharp-witted and attentive audience. The conventions of disguise and concealment, in particular, are used so extravagantly that they become parodies of the conventions, which is a sure sign of sophistication. The characters make several references to being in a play, which is another. The atmosphere is rather like that of a literary coterie, with everyone lost in admiration of his own wit and that of his close friends, and decrying the wit of others with the greatest possible malice.

What ordinarily happens in a comedy is that after certain complications a happy ending ensues, and the comedy ends in a festive occasion symbolizing the birth of a new society. This festive occasion is usually a marriage, sometimes in Shakespeare a triple or quadruple marriage. Or it may be a dance, as in the masque, or a song, as in *Love's Labour's Lost*, or a banquet, as in *The Taming of the Shrew*. The complications are usually the threats to the happiness of hero and heroine proceeding from certain blocking characters, sometimes parents, often the stock caricatures like the braggart and the pedant already mentioned. These blocking characters, because they try to frustrate the comic conclusion which the audience sees to be the desirable goal, must be presented as absurd.

In *Love's Labour's Lost* the audience is deliberately cheated of the normal comic conclusion. This fact is so obvious that the chief characters comment on it, and complain that this is not at all the way a comedy should end, with every Jack getting his appropriate Jill. The ladies promise to return a year later, but, Berowne says, "That's too long for a play." *Love's Labour's Lost* is thus the only play of Shakespeare, outside the histories, that seems to imply a sequel, and in fact that useful man Francis Meres, who supplies a full if not exhaustive list of Shakespeare's early plays, does mention a *Love's Labour's Won*. This title has been, not very convincingly, identified with one or two of the existing comedies, but it seems to me more likely to stand for the sequel which is at least hinted at in *Love's Labour's Lost*. Shakespeare doubtless never wrote such a sequel, but it is at least possible that it was promised

or announced or assumed to be forthcoming. Meres, as
his reference to the sonnets shows, knew much more
about Shakespeare than merely the names of his plays.

A dramatist may emphasize the blocking characters
who thwart the happy conclusion of the play, or he may
emphasize the conclusion itself, with all its reconcilia-
tions and last-minute fortunate discoveries. The former
is the direction of the comedy of manners, the other of
romantic comedy and of most of Shakespeare. Where
the emphasis is on the blocking characters, the tone is
satiric, and the question arises of what it is that makes
a character ridiculous. Bergson, in *Le Rire*, suggests
that an important source of laughter is the sense of
mechanism: when people are bound to an invariable
and predictable pattern of behavior they seem funny.
This conception of the ridiculous coincides with Ben
Jonson's conception of the "humor," the miser or hypo-
chondriac or fop who can behave in only one way.

In a comedy of humors one frequent action is the
release of a character from his humor. He undergoes
some experience which proves to be therapeutic, and at
the end of the play is ready to exhibit more normal
behavior. Shakespeare has such a humor comedy in *The
Taming of the Shrew*, where the cure of Katharina's
shrewishness is triumphantly demonstrated in the final
scene. There are some ambiguities: when we first see
Katharina in the play she is bullying her sister Bianca,
and when we take leave of her she is still bullying
Bianca, but has learned how to do it with social approval on her side. Still, she is cured, as far as the
dramatic action goes. Elsewhere in Shakespeare the
humor theme is often sombre or even tragic, as in

Leontes' humor of jealousy.

A comedy is usually so constructed that the blocking characters are in the ascendancy during the first part of the action, and are consequently in a position of social authority. It follows that if an individual humor is ridiculous, a humorous society is even more so. All Utopias, or schemes for making social action predictable, are objects of ridicule to comedy, and have been from Aristophanes to Gilbert and Sullivan. Hence when a comedy begins, as *Love's Labour's Lost* does, with solemn resolves "Not to see ladies, study, fast, not sleep," we realize that the direction of the comic action will be toward the breaking of these resolves. They have the place of the irrational law with which Shakespeare's comedies so often begin, like the marriage law of Athens in *A Midsummer Night's Dream* or the law of killing Syracusans in *A Comedy of Errors*.

The fact that *Love's Labour's Lost* deals with a humorous group or society means that the stock caricatures, the braggart, pedant and the rest, are not needed for the actual plot. What they form is a kind of chorus to the main action, symbolizing to some extent qualities within the King of Navarre and his courtiers. Thus when Berowne, scolding himself for falling in love, says he has been

A critic, nay, a night-watch constable,
A domineering pedant o'er the boy

he names three of the six characters as elements in his own mind. On the other side we have the theme of the "Worthies," the men of great merit enslaved by love. This theme first appears when Armado asks his page for precedents for his love and is given Hercules and Samson. It continues in Berowne's mocking speech in the fourth act with its line "To see great Hercules whipping a gig." (This reference repeats the association of the infant Hercules and Moth, who is told to go whip his gig by Holofernes.) The final appearance of the stock characters as the Worthies of course unites all of these themes.

The impetus of comedy, which moves toward the breaking of a humor or prescribed pattern of mechanical action, contains within itself its own philosophy of life, so to speak, which is not a philosophy but a refusal to be controlled by theories or logical premises at all. Thus in Rabelais, who seems to have left some traces on *Love's Labour's Lost,* including perhaps the name Holofernes, an academy is proposed which will be the exact opposite of a monastic community. The latter is founded on vows of poverty, chastity and obedience. Rabelais' Abbey of Theleme will have all its members well to do, married and doing as they like. The attitude expounded by Berowne at the beginning of the play is also that of comic pragmatism. Knowledge, Berowne implies, is not something you have but something you are: it is the art of life itself, and cannot be attained by an act of will which turns its back on life. The latter can produce only a knowledge of names, not of things.

What, then, is the particular humor that the King of Navarre's court has to be released from, corresponding to Katharina's shrewishness or Leontes' jealousy? The answer sounds difficult but is logical and simple: their humor is wit. An excess of wit, and their own pride in it, has incited them to their three-year conquest of knowledge, and Berowne, though he speaks against the retreat, is a prisoner of his own wit too. The grotesque penance imposed on him by Rosaline indicates that there is still something mechanical about his mockery, and that he cannot live up to his own precepts until he realizes that even joking is an act of communication rather than expression. Hence Berowne is an antithesis to the king's dream of esoteric knowledge, but his own wit is equally opposed to the spirit of the comic society, and equally far from "common sense" in both its Shake-spearean and its modern meanings.

A religious motive might be strong enough to keep the king and his "book-mates" at their books, but re-ligion would have to recognize the limitations of the will. There are many references in the play to the fal-lacy of achieving virtue through the will. "All pride is willing pride," the Princess says, and she also speaks of the heresy of achieving salvation by merit as "fit for these days." Berowne, too, points to the religious dimen-sion of his argument:

> For every man with his affects is born,
> Not by might mastered, but by special grace.

There are several indications that the king's "curious knotted garden" is a kind of Paradise in reverse in which, as Berowne says, what one learns is "the thing I am forbid to know."

The reason for religious language in the play is simple enough. The code of love, which eventually de-stroys the three-year pact and replaces it with a year-long service to ladies according to the rules of that code, regularly employed the language of religion. The maze of puns on "will" and "grace" relates primarily to this language, where grace means the lady's grace and will the lover's experience of need for it. The setting up of the community of study is an act of rebellious will, though the god against whom it rebels is the god of love. The plan of study is envisaged by the king as a conquest, and military metaphors suitable to intellectual "Worthies" achieving merit through their deeds occur in his opening speech. The women from France, finding themselves excluded from this garden-citadel, sit down in front of it like a besieging army. The killing of the deer by the ambushed princess is the symbol of love's victory over this benighted Eden. Holofernes, in a deliberately absurd image, compares the death of the deer to the falling of an apple from heaven to earth. The women conquer in the name of love, and impose the final commands which override all other vows.

At the same time they are caught up in the society that they conquer, and form a part of it. Under their influence the court of Navarre is transformed in the spirit of Berowne into a society of mutual mockery. This brittle and artificial society, which at such moments as the baiting of Holofernes rises into hysteria, suggests a masque like that in *The Tempest* summoned up by magic, which would dissolve at once if anyone were to speak and break the spell. The news of the death of the King of France acts in precisely this way. "Worthies, away! the scene begins to cloud," Berowne says, and the word "cloud" again seems to anticipate the great speech of Prospero on the passing of the revels which "leave not a rack behind." There are, however, two words spoken, a word of death and a word of pregnancy. Armado, who, for a conventional braggart with a Spanish name echoing "Armada" is a curiously gentle and wistful figure, then moves to the front of the action. It is he who accepts the full three-year service, he who takes on the title of "votary," and he and Jacquenetta who accomplish what there is of the normal comic resolution. It is fitting that he should be the master of ceremonies in the final moments of the play.

In many of Shakespeare's comedies the happy ending comes from what I have elsewhere called a green world, like the wood near Athens in *A Midsummer Night's Dream* or the forest of Arden in *As You Like It*. This green-world structure, where the cast disappears into a forest and straighten out all their misunderstandings there, can be seen very clearly in another early comedy, *The Two Gentlemen of Verona*. Here the happy ending is most naturally associated with seasonal symbols, with the victory of spring over winter and fertility over sterility. *Love's Labour's Lost*, which cheats us of the normal comic conclusion, moves toward a separation of the seasons. The court of Navarre complain that in the delusive perpetual spring of their contemplative retreat "Berowne is like an envious sneaping frost." Berowne accepts this, and states a preference for rolling round in earth's diurnal course. In the final scene we have the contrapuntal announcements of death and new life, already mentioned, and the two appearances of the Navarre court, first as Russians (Russia to an Elizabethan audience meant primarily cold winters) and then in their own forms. As the society breaks up and the women prepare to leave, the suspension of the normal comic close is represented by the two lovely songs of

spring and winter, where winter has the last word and
there is no suggestion of the triumph of one season over
the other. After this the two groups separate: "you that
way, we this way."

The texture of the play is a kind of symphony of
sound and imagery. The wit should perhaps be thought
of, not so much as a series of jokes punctuated by
laughs at every answer, but as verbal themes broken up
and analyzed as a composer would do in his "development." There is hardly an image in the play that is not
repeated in a different context. Even words are thus
repeated: the one exception to Berowne's resolve to
speak simply, the word "sans," has already been used by
Holofernes, so that the attentive listener's ear has been
prepared for it. Two image-themes, so to speak, are of
particular importance. One is the imagery of light and
darkness, another image from the cycle of nature re-
inforcing that of spring and winter. To this belong all
the references to the rhetoric of the eye, to love as the
sun which we do not look at but see things by, and to
the "black" Rosaline—for in Shakespeare's day "black"
meant both dark and unattractive, just as "fair" still
means both of their opposites. Hence Berowne's attempt to prove black fair shows a mastery of paradox
which is useful when his friends need proof that breaking their vows is really a sign of fidelity. The other
thematic image is that of number, which brings out the
affinity of *Love's Labour's Lost* to the masque and the
dance. Moth's little rhyme with its "envoy" (which in
turn contains a polyglot pun on "oie," goose) sets up an
echo of three and four in our ears against the groups of
three and four among the lovers: "four woodcocks in a

dish," and the like. The nine Worthies repeat the number of the eight lovers with the somewhat ambiguous Boyet as a connecting link.

The variety of verse forms in the play, quatrains, couplets, blank verse, sonnets, lyrics, and even a passage in anapests, can hardly be missed; nor can the variety of language, from the pedantries of Holofernes and Armado to the bucolic dialect of Dull and Costard. Holofernes is of particular interest to the student of language. The words "debt" and "doubt" came originally from French, and Chaucer spells them, quite correctly, "dette" and "doute." But in Shakespeare's day along came people like Holofernes, insisting that b's should be inserted in them to show their Latin origin in debito and dubito, and we have been stuck with those b's ever since. Holofernes even tries to pronounce the b's, and others of his kind succeeded in making us say "perfect," where Chaucer said "perfit." Here is a change in the language which Shakespeare's sharp ear and eye caught and recorded in its passing. The general impression that *Love's Labour's Lost* makes on us is one of tremendous buoyancy and exuberance, as one of the world's greatest masters of words begins to feel something of the real range of his strength and skill.

QUESTIONS FROM THE FLOOR

Q. Is there not a more explicitly religious aspect to the play than you suggest?

A. I am speaking of its centre of gravity, so to speak. Writers of comedies in Shakespeare's day were not supposed to discuss religion; they were supposed to provide what we call love interest. But of course such

verbal constructs as the language of courtly love can
provide a series of receding planes, and what plane
you stop at may be to some extent a matter of choice.
Q. Would you connect Rosaline with the dark lady of
the sonnets?
A. Some of the sonnets are very similar in tone to
Love's Labour's Lost, but most are bitterer and more
sombre. The dark lady at times is like something out of
Proust, and her claim to the title of lady seems to me
more precarious than Rosaline's.
Q. But there is bitterness in Berowne's references to
her willingness to "do the deed," and the like. If *Love's
Labour's Lost* and the dark-lady sonnets were written
roughly around the same time, as seems probable, do not
we ascribe too much versatility to Shakespeare's experience in endeavouring to separate them?
A. Berowne pretends to be bitter when he is scolding
himself; when his friends speak in dispraise of Rosaline
he reacts very differently. I am not happy about trying
to align the sonnets with Shakespeare's experience;
they were produced, not by Shakespeare's experience,
but by his imagination. And with an imagination so
powerful the merest hint of experience, even in someone else, would be enough to go on.
Q. What is the point of "honorificabilitudinitatibus"?
A. It was the longest word known in Latin, and occurs
elsewhere—I think in a play of Marston's. Very long
words, unless technical terms, can really be used only
in a comic context, and a proverbially long word is
always good for a laugh.

Michael Langham was appointed Artistic Director of the Stratford Festival in 1955. In addition to the planning of the Festival as a whole he has continued as a stage director and his productions of ten of the plays presented in the last six seasons have been among the most notable of Stratford's successes. In 1960 he directed *Love's Labour's Lost* and *Coriolanus*. Born in England he was trained initially as a student of law but was already acting and directing when his career was interrupted by the War; in 1946 he was appointed Assistant Director to Beatrix Lehmann at the Arts Council Midland Theatre Company. In 1949 he became Director of Productions at the Birmingham Repertory Theatre and the following year saw the first of many productions for the Royal Shakespeare Theatre in Stratford-upon-Avon. In addition to his work in Britain and Canada he has directed productions in Belgium, Holland, and Australia as well as at the Edinburgh and Berlin Festivals.

MICHAEL LANGHAM

AN APPROACH TO STAGING

Shakespeare's works

The subject of staging Shakespeare is vast, and in the time at my disposal I can only hope to indicate some random impressions of my own regarding it: no more than that. Maybe this is just as well. It is advisable, I believe, to avoid discussing or dwelling upon the works of the Great Masters at any considerable length. They are demanding companions, and easily become a hazardous obsession: Shakespeare especially. His Kingdom often contains a mysterious darkness. Despite the fact that it has been so written up in hand books, so trodden down by tourists, so provided with beaten roads and sign posts and official guides, it is nevertheless a region full of dark pitfalls for the mind, of tangled thickets of textual interpretation, of mazes of thought in which many wander and find no issue, and of many paths whitened by the bleaching bones of critics. It is, in short, a highly dangerous region, fit only for those enjoying the most robust mental health. Indeed, of the inhabitants of the insane asylums in Great Britain it has been calculated that, after religious maniacs, the two next largest classes consist of those who rave about the Royal Family, and those who, by pondering too deeply the ways of Shakespeare, have quite unhinged their minds. Let us therefore examine, from a discreet distance, the problem of getting up a Shakespeare play and putting it on the stage.

First — and this is not idle flippancy — should it be put on the stage at all?

Ever since Shakespeare wrote the plays, there have always been a select few who have believed them better read than seen. At the end of the last century and the beginning of this one — no doubt aggravated by the over-elaborate naturalism of productions such as Beer-bohm Tree's — this attitude became a positive doctrine. Far better, these people maintained, to see the plays in the theatre of the mind, where the imagination could range freely, where there was no danger of conflict between the preconception of the spectator and that of the performers, where there was no possibility of being frustrated by production budgets, or of being tripped up by tedious practical problems of staging. When it was pointed out to this élite few that Shakespeare wrote solely for the theatre, that he never considered his works as Literature, that he never showed the smallest interest in having them published, and that, in fact, we only possess them through the loyal offices of two members of his company who collected and edited the Folio from a lot of battered and dog-eared old prompt scripts, their attitude remained quite unshaken. "Had Shake-speare lived in some later age," these specially en-lightened connoisseurs replied, "he would certainly not have written for the theatre; his talents would have found their reward in some other way. He chose to write for the theatre because, to put it bluntly, he needed the money; he was determined to improve the family fortunes, and, in the Elizabethan age, the theatre provided the most lucrative return for his peculiar gifts. So it was for the Globe Theatre that he wrote. 'His great soul,' Carlyle says, 'had to crush itself, as best it could, into that and no other mould.' But his genius greatly outgrew the confines of the Globe, and we can best appreciate him when we can emancipate him, as by reading we can emancipate him, altogether from the theatre."

This was their attitude. Today, such voices are few, but they can still be heard, despite the fact that over the last sixty years the quest for the essential Shakespeare in the theatre has been more hotly pursued than at any other time since he wrote.

How is this freakish, "stay at home" attitude towards Shakespeare best answered? It is akin to finding more satisfaction in reading an orchestral score than in hearing it performed as the composer intended. Further, it concedes only a negligible standing to the interpretive arts; it ignores the possible genius of the performer. And, undeniably, some performers have proved great illuminators of scores; they have even been known to enrich them beyond the composer's range.

Secondly, this "keep-Shakespeare-out-of-the-theatre" brigade ignores how the works came to be created.

The two chief partners in drama are the dramatist and the actor. It was not until the 1570's when the hitherto rambling theatrical companies settled for the first time in London, when they acquired, for the first time in the history of the English tongue, theatres — homes of their own; it was not until the dramatist could thus keep in constant touch with the actors, not until tomorrow's work could truly be said to have profited by today's, that a close creative collaboration between dramatist and actor came about. They saw into each other's task deeper and deeper. And out of this partnership there developed a vital—and with Shakespeare at his greatest—a great art: the art of creating and interpreting character. It is important to remember that Shakespeare happened to be there at the moment of this discovery, and that it *was* a discovery. It was blazingly new; before this, figures in plays had either been walking abstractions or animated lay figures. But here was a new invigorating force in the theatre, and Shakespeare quickly became its leading exponent.

This discovery, born of the collaboration between dramatist and actor, led in time to yet another discovery — the one which turned Shakespeare from a good dramatist into a great one: that the outward clashing of character with character is poor theatrical material when compared with the conflict that could be shown as taking place within the fermenting spirit of one man. Isolate this man in his surroundings — as Shakespeare does with all his tragic heroes — confine him within alien circumstances and wills, and see what happens. See how he will quicken and grow.

It was a discovery due to be made in England at the time of Shakespeare's life. The Renaissance in Europe had set it spiritually free. It was due to be made too in terms of drama, for in drama, as in no other art, there existed the necessary medium of living breathing man, primed to communicate all his yearnings and frustrations and joys and miseries and confusions, directly and with no barriers, to his fellow breathing men. Further, this had to be a poet's discovery, for in what else than poetry could one hope to paint, not men's thoughts and emotions merely, but their very souls. Shakespeare, working with his actors, set out to do this. The Greeks had done it before him, but he and his colleagues were to find their own way, through trial and error. A full realization of this spectacular feat can only be achieved by experiencing the performance of the plays in the theatre.

If then there is a good argument for staging Shakespeare's works, how is this best to be done?

Can tradition guide us?

Every other theatrical inheritance, such as the Kabuki theatre of Japan or the Classical theatre of France, enjoys a direct link with its roots through tradition. Theatrical tradition, of course, is not written down; it is passed on only by continuing practice, by custom, by each generation adopting through selective imitation the ways of its predecessors. But most links with the tradition of Shakespeare's theatre were lost when the Puritans closed the playhouses in England for nearly twenty years. The custom was thus broken, and when theatrical activity was permitted again at the restoration of the Monarchy in 1660, there was no looking to the past for guidance, but to the present, to the then flourishing theatre of Paris and Molière. And this demanded a very different kind of theatrical convention from Shakespeare's. Consequently the tradition of his theatre tumbled almost entirely into oblivion. When you hear people speak nowadays of "traditional Shakespeare acting," they are really referring to the results of an unnatural tradition having been imposed upon the works at the end of the seventeenth century: so ill did it fit them that during the next two centuries—and particularly the nineteenth—it became utterly bastardized.

As far as I know, no other theatrical heritage is in a similar plight. Even the revolution in Russia did not destroy traditions of theatrical practice there. Admittedly these traditions do not go very far back, but I was nevertheless surprised to discover at a recent performance of an Ostrovsky play in Moscow that, despite the Marxist attempt to stamp out all aristocratic sympathies, not only the older actors, but also the young ones of 19 or 20 years, were able to portray finely-etched, nineteenth-century, aristocratic characters in a manner that all of us could find both human and sympathetic.

For over 300 years Shakespeare has been performed in theatres not only different from that for which he wrote, but architecturally at odds with his intentions. Even the great Memorial shrine at Stratford-upon-Avon, in spite of vast expenditure over frequent reconstructions of its stage, remains a most unsuitable, unhelpful building for producing Shakespeare's works.

This theatre, in Stratford, Ontario, whose influence is gradually creeping into various parts of the Western world including Stratford-upon-Avon, represents an attempt to get back to the essential elements of Shakespeare's stagecraft, in the hope that through trial and error we may be able to rediscover the heart of his theatrical genius and thus bridge the gap created by the damnable Puritans. Since we do not know for certain exactly what his theatre was like—the few surviving drawings of Elizabethan playhouses leave room for almost limitless conjecture—we are forced to indulge in much guess-work regarding it. We have, in truth, no conclusive proof that his stage was three-sided: it may have been, as Dr. Hotson argues persuasively in his recent book, four-sided. Even so, I am convinced from the experience I have been lucky enough to enjoy with this stage that his plays were written for a structure much more like this than the conventional picture-frame theatre.

The conventional theatre is usually rectangular with the audience at one end and the stage at the other. The stage is fronted by an arch, usually decorated to represent a picture frame, behind which the actors face their customers over an orchestra pit and a highly symbolical barrier of footlights—similar to the green baize door which in old country houses separates the servants' quarters from the masters'. And the customers see their actors framed, as it were, in another world. They do not imagine this world; they see it. It is the world of scenery and scenic illusion. Even when the "setting" is of the least representational character—even when it consists solely of black tabs—it remains a scenic illusion: a framed picture enclosing the actors and perforce contributing to the meaning and experience of the play.

In Shakespeare's theatre, there was no picture frame, and hence no scenic illusion. Illusion was purely in the actor, and was achieved by the creation of a strong imaginative bond between him and his audience. The aim seems to have been to awaken the utmost imaginative response; there were no distractions—like scenery, which more often deadens rather than stimulates the imagination. Usually, in Shakespeare's plays, the whereabouts of the characters at any given point is quite unimportant. When it is important, the author puts the necessary information into the mouth of one of his actors. In his theatre the scene could thus be switched from street to council chamber, from cave to battlefield, and from ship to garden without pausing to change and establish a totally superfluous scenic illusion.

Secondly, the conventional stage is two-dimensional —like a framed picture. It is difficult for actors to give more than two-dimensional performances on it. They have to *pretend* to play to each other, while really playing to the audience, and this leads, perforce, to rather shallow relationships between characters. Shakespeare's theatre on the other hand was three-dimensional, not only in its physical arrangement, but also, presumably, in its acting, its movement and its design. The actors were grouped, I believe, in semi-circular patterns to face one another, not the audience. The effect of this, in my experience, was not to exclude the audience but to involve them more fully in the experience of the play, and, of course, to deepen the relationship between the characters.

The philosophy of this Canadian Stratford is something like this: if you will work with the actors they will create for you the totality of life. This stage will not be some literal, fixed location, but at any given moment will constitute the crucible in which the living elements of the play will interact. We do not ask our audiences to believe that what they are seeing is really taking place, as in real life. We ask them to indulge with us in the game of make-believe, but to retain sufficient objectivity to be conscious of the parallel between real life and this heightened ritualistic performance of it.

We do not try to encourage as great a degree of objectivity as did the late Berthold Brecht. He worked specifically to alienate his audiences from the experience of a play. He insisted that it should at all times be made apparent to them that they were not witnessing real events happening before their eyes *at that very moment,* but were sitting in a theatre where the director had striven to produce, by all the means at his disposal, effects that would keep the audience separated, estranged and alienated from the actors. He wished to alienate his audience in order to educate it; if he could persuade people that what was happening was not true inside the playhouse, but was true *outside* it, he had achieved the result he was seeking.

As I see it, the convention of Shakespeare's theatre, and the one to which we are aspiring in this theatre, is not as radical as Brecht's, but it is certainly in a similar direction—though we do not presume to set ourselves up to educate. We aim simply to evoke as much in our audiences as we can evoke, and as much as they are capable of giving.

How does a director prepare to put a Shakespeare play on the stage?

There are no rules, there is no one right way. Directors differ in their approach to a production, much as actors do towards a part. Some will leap at an immediate broad impression, and then gradually trim it and discipline it. Others will seek for the smallest hint of the *essence* of a work, and, having found it, expand

and build on it. My approach is usually the latter.

Clearly the text needs careful study: it needs to be read many times (though first impressions are always significant). One is, of course, distracted by the incomprehensible passages, and driven for help to the glossaries and notes. (Frequently the notes themselves are incomprehensible and cry out for further notes!) One of the first impressions arising from these readings will be that of the story. Shakespeare's stories, more often than not, are thoroughly far-fetched, and one may wonder how an audience can be induced to swallow them. Then, perhaps, a light dawns, and one realizes they are not meant to be regarded literally. A profound writer will invariably choose a narrative that has a profound human appeal for him, and often such narratives will be based on myth or legend, and, for all the human wisdom a myth or a legend contains, it is usually a highly romanticized affair, and only acceptable if presented in a highly romanticized manner. I do not mean to suggest that all the plays are based on myth or legend, but many of them are. The Histories certainly are not, nor, for that matter, are they history lessons; in them the narrative simply serves as a structure within which the author weaves and spins his themes and reveals his characters.

The next striking impression may well be the style of the writing. An appreciation of this may provide a key to the style of acting needed for the play—to the style of production. After reading a number of Shakespeare's plays, one realizes they have many quite divergent styles. Compare Molière and Racine, even Aeschylus and Sophocles, and for that matter, all the great novel-

ists, and one finds these writers have a uniformity of
style, and tone. A character or a scene from one of their
works might appear without any shock to our sense of
tone in any of the others. A director who can master
successfully one of Molière's plays can feel confident
about directing any of them. Not so with Shakespeare.
He is a master of many styles and each of his great plays
possesses its own atmosphere and colour. Even the two
fairy plays: the silvery moonlight of the *Dream* is very
different from the faint haze of enchantment which envelops *The Tempest*. And every one of his tragedies
differs from all the others: *Romeo* glows with the rich-
ness of Giorgione; *Lear* is cold and dark and envelops
its dim-lit scenes with a kind of winter mist; it would be
impossible to imagine the cliff scene from *Lear* transferred into the glare of *Othello;* while to pass from
Julius Caesar to *Antony and Cleopatra* is like passing
from a gallery of antique sculpture to a great palace
rich with Titians and Paul Veronese frescoes. That the
painter of one of these scenes should be the painter of
the others seems a constantly repeated marvel. If we
should find that the pictures of Giorgione, Raphael,
Michaelangelo, Titian and Veronese had all been
painted by one hand we could hardly be more astonished.

In searching for the essential style, or character, taste
and essence of a Shakespeare play, we are best advised
to examine carefully the form of its writing. The Elizabethan age was passionately musical—indeed, musical
virtuosity at that time was probably a more valuable
social asset than literacy—and it is folly not to regard
the texts primarily as musical scores. The Elizabethans,

with no dramatic heritage to guide them, but with the air of adventure and discovery that distinguished their time, seem to have experimented vigorously with all possible forms of dialogue—rhyming verse, blank verse, the longer line, the shorter line, prose—like a painter choosing and mixing his colours, until they found the exact answer to suit their various dramatic needs.

They seem most often to have used prose for an informal effect, as in the domestic atmosphere of *Much Ado* and the pastoral informality of *As You Like It,* or for a comic one—Shakespeare's greatest comic creation, Falstaff, was made up entirely of prose—or simply as a contrast to verse; after a scene of soaring emotional verse, or even of measured contemplative verse, it is effective to drop suddenly into lower-tempered, businesslike prose. However, they seemed to find that it lacked the exhilaration and the music of verse—both valuable dramatic qualities in themselves—and that it was harder to speak: harder to speak, that is, than the simple forthright verse which swings along to a uniform cadence and tune. Also, for dramatic purposes, they seemed to find it harder to write—harder to write well, at any rate.

Verse was generally preferred. But was it to be blank or rhymed? Rhyme can give a certain snap to repartee: if spoken quickly enough it can make an otherwise puerile remark sound really quite clever. Moreover, it adds tune, keeps a scene in shape, and drives the action forward with both swing and charm. Shakespeare used it a lot in his early plays—it was probably more in vogue then, and he was still proving himself—but he never used it by rule, always for dramatic effect. In *Romeo*

and Juliet, for example, after the hot-bloody street
brawl, after the fussings and bustlings of Capulet
launching his daughter's "coming-out" ball, after the
colourful swirl of the over-crowded dance, Shakespeare
brings his two lovers together with a hushed, still simplicity: the first lines they exchange take the form of a
sonnet. This was no charming literary whim, but a
consciously devised theatrical effect. But rhyme has the
drawback of being inflexibly tramelled by its form. It
does not lend itself to a variety of *tempi* or emotions;
nor, above all, does it lend itself to characterization.

Blank verse clearly had the better of it, and the ten-
syllable line won the day. I will confine myself to men-
tioning one important consideration concerning it.
Dramatic verse should be no more awkward to speak
than should vocal music be awkward to sing. If it is, we
write the composer down as incompetent. So we should
the dramatist. But there is nothing to stop the composer or the dramatist trying his performer's skill to the
utmost—as Marlowe tried the skill of his leading player,
Edward Alleyn. Alleyn must have possessed not only
incredible breath control but also an amazingly re-
sourceful and powerful vocal organ, for it is most unlikely that Marlowe would have continued to make
demands in his scripts that could not be met on the
stage. (I know of no contemporary actor who can fully
master these big vocal extravagancies.) Shakespeare
himself threw out similar challenges to the voice —
especially to his highly trained boy actors: there are
passages for Juliet, for instance, which are as deliberately bravura as an aria of Mozart's.

The modern actor—and director, for that matter—

inhibited by an overabundance of naturalism, tends on the whole either to shirk these highly-coloured musical-emotional climaxes (sometimes by destroying their true quality through shapeless underplaying, sometimes by cutting them) or to present them with a loud, *empty*, rhetorical flourish. It is perhaps a reflection of this age that our actors and we in the audience seem to have lost the appetite for the big dramatic aria where a "larger than life" hero or heroine faces a "larger than life" conflict. We have not lost this appetite in the opera house: indeed, we should be grossly affronted if an opera singer *hummed* his great aria. But such avoidance of the task set is—to our great loss—what we regularly tolerate in the "straight" theatre. In my view it has grown too straight, flat, "natural," and musically un-stimulating. The contemporary player, and especially the conscientious seeker after the "truth" of a part, is so preoccupied with this truth in his own small, domestic terms, that he continually overlooks and belittles his author's vaster intentions. He resists at all cost the "un-natural," while important theatre, almost invariably, can only hope to convey its widest implications by eschewing natural-ness—as in the Moscow Art Theatre's current productions of Checkov. Many of our modern actors prefer to drop down on all fours, to scratch and to grunt inarticulately, than to reach out and up and beyond to the world of the gods.

Our society, which we may call a society of disillu-sion, is no doubt responsible for this. In the past man has always been ready to respond to a deep-rooted impulse to glory in his creation and his destiny. Indeed, out of this impulse he has often aspired to a kind of divinity. In our society today, moral values and faith being in short supply, he is generally cynical about such things. The astronomer-scientist almost alone finds a glory in his destiny: he has faith that all will be revealed; he keeps his head lifted to the stars, and finds a concrete meaning in Heaven. But western man, not truly understanding the mysteries of science (the interpreters—the poets, novelists and playwrights—have not yet enlightened him), and having lost much of his faith, not only in a loving Heavenly Father but also, and perhaps more importantly, in Man himself, generally sees no point in dwelling on the glory of anything.

One manifestation of this is the "beatnik"; another may often be found in the theatre, when an actor, made cynical and grasping by an over-materialistic, disillusioned society, falls back upon his diminished view of himself to measure the great roles of Macbeth or Lear or Othello. Naturally enough, he finds himself "o'er-parted," and so trims and hacks away at the role until he can fit it to his own puny stature. Insignificant, domestic themes are then made to take the place of the play's major timeless issues.

What is to be done? We cannot put the clock back. But we can, in the theatre as in the other performing arts, struggle to retain our values and cling to a strength and a truth in our interpretation of the classics. We can surely use our gifts to enhance these works rather than to diminish them. We may fail ever so little or ever so much, but I think if we are deeply aware of the significance to us of their timeless universality *before* their immediate, contemporary implications, we can hope to maintain their true stature.

But back to our search for the essence of a Shakespeare play in the form of the writing. (The French would say—in fact they do say—that Shakespeare had no form; but I am concerned with comparing his works with each other: not him with other artists.) In his early plays the form is comparatively obvious, rigid and strong; he seems to be consciously working at it— often, as in *Love's Labour's Lost*, delighting in it for its own sake. At this point in his career, a display of virtuosity with form seems to have been the fashion, and Shakespeare was concerned initially, we may suppose, with establishing himself as a fashionable playwright. Rather than bringing his principal characters vividly to life as individuals—a task to which he was already well fitted: witness the lesser people in these early works, the clowns and the eccentrics—he saddled these principals with the inhibiting responsibility of carrying the plot along in the appropriate musical form. This form, which may swing from a sequence of the strictest blank verse to a sequence of rhymed couplets to a sequence of very balanced prose and on to a sequence of quatrains, a musical phrase with the climax or punctuation after the fourth line: this form represents a firm musical pattern. The author has knowingly shaped his dialogue into a set kind of tune which it is folly to ignore, for the formal style of writing is so pronounced as to be unactable and unenjoyable unless presented with an equally pronounced formal style of speaking and staging.

This applies to his "apprentice" works. Later this single-minded concern for form diminishes as his concern for characterization grows. The verse becomes freer and richer, and its form less evident—and there-

fore of less guidance to a director in search of an appropriate style. Indeed, as we study Shakespeare's works
chronologically, their form becomes steadily more and
more elusive—as if the author were by now only sub-
consciously aware of it—while their themes, their
characters and their atmospheres grow more vivid and
powerful and often larger than life. The style of acting
and production now is harder to determine. With the
tragedies, for instance, the director's skill is severely
tried, for not only is their style evasive, but the works
themselves are so huge and awesome that it is well-nigh
impossible to master them. It is small consolation for
the director to realize that a great dramatic masterpiece
will inevitably reveal much of its splendour and power
in performance no matter how paltry his contribution
may be. Often—too often in my experience as a director
and as a member of the audience—he will find his production drifting into a heavy, realistic, melodramatic
style which he did not intend. He will find further that
by aiming with his actors at a "larger-than-life" scale
of performance all subtlety has been thumped out of
existence—and Shakespeare at his greatest, with all his
stops out, remains, in my view, always the subtlest of
writers. Frankly, I have never seen (I have certainly
never directed) a performance of a Shakespearean
tragedy which even began to match the stupendous
aspirations of the text.

With these later works the decisive clue to discover-
ing the essence and style required in performance
surely lies in the matter of 'content': the theme — or
rather, the themes—the characters, the imagery, the
atmosphere created by everything in the story or legend,

the scale of its writing.

A director will probably ask himself, "What impression is this intended to make? What sort of emotional experience is meant to be stimulated by it?" And finally the leading and sometimes dangerous question, "What is the play about?" He should be aware that his answer to this last will change over the years as he himself will change and develop, and also that in answering it he may strive, perhaps too hard, for an "overall-concept." He may, for example, be excited to find an answer which neatly fits eighty per cent of the play, and then, thrilled by the notion of accomplishing a really definitive production of a great classic, he may be sorely tempted to impose a distorted interpretation on the remaining twenty per cent in order to bring it into line. Yet the question must be asked — and answered; but with discretion, with great discretion, because Shakespeare is not one of those writers who establishes a point of view in one work and then repeats and expands it in the next. In fact, you can never be sure that you know what his point of view is. With the possible exception of a recurring and growing insistence on the superiority of the female over the male, he seems to be forever changing his attitudes and shifting his ground. It was on this account that Bernard Shaw called him "muddle-headed." If we look closely at his writings, we find no consistent attitude towards philosophy or politics or any major topic—which is why, I suppose, he has become the particular prophet of almost every sect of worshippers, philosophers and politicians. Saint and devil now vie in quoting him to their purpose. He has given to every type of person the perfect line with which to summarize, excuse or extol the drift of his opinion and the practice of his life. The truth is that he was not concerned with stating a point of view; he was not concerned with saying "this is right" and "that is wrong"; he was concerned with saying simply, "this is life, this is human nature." To impose on him the function of a stern but benevolent Teacher is grossly to misrepresent the man.

In my view the most rewarding approach, in apprais- ing what these works are about, is that of the humanist. But I think it needs to be at once both detached and compassionate, never prejudiced, or sentimental, always seeking for those illuminating human truths which, coupled with the poetry, represent the heart of the work. There is, of course, a danger that such an ap- proach will lead to the realistic human values gaining more attention than the poetic—which is folly, for the poetic values have in the theatre the power to create an experience of sublime human ecstasy, and are unques- tionably more important. But, conversely, emphasizing them to the point of excluding the human values seems equally misguided. Ideally, I think, there should be a delicate blending of the two, and this will prove a highly precarious operation.

In what little space remains, I must turn from theorizing to more practical matters. In my view—and it is purely a personal view and in no way representative of a great body of opinion—all the considerations that I have mentioned, and more, are essential before a direc- tor can even begin to think about casting a Shakespeare play. After such sobering reflection, either he will want to throw in the sponge, or he will know what kind of

actors he requires, what balance of voices is most suitable—where a tenor voice is called for, where a bass,
and so on—what variety of physique would be effective,
and which characters have got to spark off each other
and therefore need to be played by actors possessing in
their personalities the potential for a highly-charged
chemical conflict.

It should now be clear what style of acting is required: artificial comedy (the most difficult since it
demands the most craft), rich realism, high romantic,
tender lyrical, high heroic. It should also be clear to
what extent the style fluctuates within the play. Nowadays in Shakespearean productions, directors seem
over-keen to smooth everything into an unchanging
unity of style, thereby ignoring the rich and colourful
variety for which the author has planned.

The movement or choreography of the play may also
be taking on patterns by now in the director's mind: he
will begin to know whether it is to be sparse and strong
and austere, or lustily energetic and angular, or fluid
and decorative and softly rounded.

Gradually the design of the production will start to
emerge: it will represent an attempt to add through
colour, line, movement and grouping a suitably evoca-
tive meaning to the play's flavour and style. The de-
signer will be called in—and probably offer much helpful stimulus—the question of costumes will be discussed,
the period will be chosen. As each period possesses a
distinctive style of its own, a suitable choice is of the
utmost importance.

Since this matter of period is rather controversial, I
am going to conclude this talk with some detailed

comment on it. I do not propose to try and deal with the designing of picture-frame sets for Shakespeare, because in this wonderful theatre the problem fortunately does not arise!

In Shakespeare's playhouse his works were performed in contemporary dress: it was often splendidly extravagant dress, but (with the possible exception of *Henry VIII*—no doubt some early Tudor wardrobe was still lying around) always contemporary. Even when the plays were set in some earlier period of history, like *Julius Caesar, King Lear,* or *Macbeth,* it is thought most improbable that any more than a mild acknowledgement was paid to the period in question. The characters were always *recognizable* characters to the Elizabethans. No distracting barrier in terms of dress was placed between this audience and their experience of the play. It might seem good sense for us, then, to follow suit and present the works in our own modern dress. Such a plan has, of course, been put into action frequently by each succeeding age, including our own, ever since Shakespeare wrote, and often with exciting results, for many hitherto unsuspected meanings in the texts and in the relationships of characters were suddenly and startlingly illuminated. But the drawback to this policy is, I think, twofold. First, it produces a disturbing conflict between dress and speech—a problem which never arose with the Elizabethans; to them the speech was as contemporary as were the clothes. Secondly, modern dress tends to encourage the introduction of modern trappings, such as telephones, bicycles, motor cars, cigarettes, chewing gum, etc., which, for all the 'quaint' amusement they supply, are both fussy and distracting and easily lead to a belittling of the play's main themes. There are many eminent figures in the theatre today who believe that as Shakespeare's mind was so essentially a product of the Renaissance, modern productions of his plays should always be set within hailing distance of that period of history.

Personally, apart from not being able to discern any advantage in transplanting the Histories out of their true period, I have an open mind on the subject. I believe that as long as a director resists the temptation to turn a Shakespearean production into an excuse for a fancy dress ball, and as long as he honestly believes his designs preserve and enhance the essence of the work and place the minimum barrier between his audience and the genius of Shakespeare, little else matters.

I began this talk by pointing out that many of the more ardent worshippers at Shakespeare's Shrine suffer, in consequence, varying degrees of mental derangement. I must confess I put this in largely as a "go slow" warning to myself. Now that I have said my piece, it may be all too obvious that I qualify as one of the Dotty Bardolaters. If so, there is little I can do about it. I have capitulated to the sickness quite involuntarily, and I am happily confident that it is incurable.

Let me close by exhorting all those amongst us who are fellow-invalids to LUXURIATE with me in the Malady, while I admonish, with a pertinent misquotation, all those amongst us who have sworn a defiant Oath to resist it:

"You must now lose your oath to find yourselves,
    Or else you'll lose yourselves to keep your oath."

NORTHROP FRYE

The tragedies of
nature and fortune

In my first lecture I said that in the earlier period of
Elizabethan drama comedy was better supplied than
tragedy with models and precedents. Tragedy had
Seneca, whose plays may not have been intended for
the stage at all, and Seneca bequeathed ghosts, revenge
plots, much impressive rhetoric, and mythological
themes. The earlier writers of tragedy learned some of
their structural principles from writing historical plays,
and historical plays had inherited more directly the
medieval conception of tragedy. In the Middle Ages
tragedy was thought of not dramatically but as a certain
kind of narrative, dealing normally with the fall of a
man in high place. In *The Canterbury Tales*, for example, the monk is a jovial person from whom the Host
clearly expects a ribald story. But as soon as he is asked
for a tale he remembers that he is a cleric and a scholar,
gives an academic definition of tragedy and proceeds
to tell us a long series of tragic *exempla*, as they were
called, starting from the falls of Lucifer and Adam and
working his way down until the knight breaks in with
an impatient protest that the company has heard
enough dismal tales.

Chaucer's successor Lydgate, not having any knight
to stop him, amassed a huge collection of such stories
called *The Falls of Princes*, and Lydgate was followed
in the sixteenth century by *The Mirror for Magistrates*,
which also grew to enormous proportions. Clearly there
was a demand among middle-class readers for accounts
of disaster in high places. The conception of tragedy
presented by these stories was symbolized by the wheel
of fortune, a symbol which goes back to Boethius in the
fifth century and is illustrated everywhere in medieval
poetry and painting.

The history play does not need to be as tightly constructed as the tragedy or the comedy. The continuity
in history itself gives the history play something of that
processional and sequential structure which is the
natural form of all primitive drama, from medieval
Biblical plays to *The Canvas Barricade*. We can see this
processional structure in many early Elizabethan plays
such as Marlowe's *Tamburlaine*, and *Henry VIII*, late
in the Shakespeare canon as it is, preserves it more
clearly than any other of Shakespeare's histories. Here
there is a series of three falls, those of Buckingham, of
Wolsey, and of Catherine of Aragon, and these tragedies are *exempla* of a process which has been going on
in history ever since the original fall of Satan, who set
the pattern:

And when he falls, he falls like Lucifer,
Never to hope again.

The wheel of fortune is a tragic conception, though
it is possible to get a technically comic conclusion by
stopping the wheel turning halfway. This happens at

least twice in Shakespeare's histories, in *Henry V* and
again in *Henry VIII*. *Henry V* ends with the king master
of France and about to marry the French princess. Yet
the ending is still tragic by implication, for Henry died
almost immediately and sixty years of unbroken disaster followed for England. If anyone did not know
that, after Shakespeare had written four plays to describe it, there was still the epilogue of *Henry V* to remind him. *Henry VIII* also has a technically comic conclusion: as Buckingham, Wolsey and Catherine go down
on the wheel, Anne Boleyn, Cromwell and Cranmer
come up, and the play ends with their triumph. But,
again, everyone knows that the wheel will go on turning, that Anne Boleyn and Cromwell will go to the
block in their turn and Cranmer to the stake. Thus the
play is, again, tragic by implication, which is one reason
why it was called by Sir Henry Wotton "All Is True,"
and why the prologue warns us that a deeply serious
play is to follow.

The action of *Henry VIII* shows the king gradually
coming into focus as the centre of the play. At the
beginning he is under Wolsey's spell, ready to believe
that Buckingham is a traitor when Buckingham is clearly nothing of the kind. But he gradually gets more
control and more insight into the intrigues of his court,
and at the end of the play he is completely master of
the dramatic situation. What we see in him at the end
of the play is an incarnation of Fortune, the power that
turns fortune's wheel, raising those who are low and
casting down those who are high. Being a strong king,
he turns the wheel himself, and is not, like Richard II,
turned by it. Opposite fortune is a hidden providence,

which never appears in the superficial actions of history, and yet is there, an omnipotent and ruthless power ready to tear the whole social and religious structure of the nation to pieces in order to get Queen Elizabeth born. These two polarized forces of providence and fortune make up the action of the play: a simple, almost naive action, yet one ideally suited to a processional and pageant-like history.

If we look at the spacing of histories in the Shakespearean canon we may be a little puzzled. Shakespeare starts out full of enthusiasm for the history play, and writes six of them early in his career. But after *Henry V* he seems to lose interest in the form, and to return to it only at the very end, and then in a play which many people have difficulty in believing is wholly his. Yet, if we think of what British history meant to the Elizabethan audience, his interest in history is more consistent than at first appears. British history in Shakespeare's day did not begin with Julius Caesar and 55 B.C.; it began with the Trojan War, after which Aeneas founded Rome and his descendant Brutus founded a kingdom in Britain. Rome was a second Troy, and Britain, after a Welsh dynasty had risen with the Tudors, would become a third Troy, growing to greatness as Rome declined. We notice that around the turn of the century, when Shakespeare is busy with the *Henry IV* and *V* sequence, he writes a play on the Trojan war, *Troilus and Cressida*, which shows the pro-Trojan and anti-Greek bias that we should expect. He also begins a series of Roman plays, and another series associated with British history before the time of King John. Lear is an ancient king of Britain; Macbeth belongs to early

Scotland; Hamlet is connected with the period of
Danish ascendancy over England. The double series is
concluded by *Cymbeline,* where British and Roman
themes are both prominent, and the two peoples recon-
ciled in the final scene.

In the Roman plays Shakespeare was dealing with
the fortunes of a cousin nation, an older civilization than
his own, in many respects more like ours than like his—
a fact which the present production of *Coriolanus* attempts to symbolize in its costuming. Dictatorships,
annihilation wars, world-states struggling for suprem-
acy, are familiar to us, but they must have stretched even
Shakespeare's imagination to its limits. In most of the
tragedies, while Shakespeare is dramatically impartial,
there is no real division of moral sympathies. It would
be merely perverse to take sides with Goneril and Regan
against Cordelia, or with Iago against Desdemona, and
even with Macbeth and Claudius it is impossible to
regard their crucial acts as anything but simply crimes.
But the assassination of Caesar, the suicide of Cleopatra,
the banishment of Coriolanus, are scenes in which we
feel a division of moral sympathies in ourselves, and
they reflect a theoretical and self-conscious approach
to social issues which is more Roman and modern than
it is primarily Elizabethan. True, we find this division
of moral sympathies in other plays—*Richard II,* for
instance—but it is in the three Roman plays that it
seems to affect the structure of the dramatic conflict
most deeply.

The source of *Coriolanus* is of course Plutarch, and
what Plutarch's life of Coriolanus most naturally suggests is a class melodrama with Coriolanus as the villain.

In Plutarch the grievances of the people are much more specific and justifiable than they are in Shakespeare. Shakespeare omits a highly significant passage in Plutarch about the rapacity of money-lenders, and allows his citizens little more than an aimless and sullen grousing. Again, Plutarch's Coriolanus is more calculating: his speech to the senate strikes us as prepared and coldly malignant, and there is little in it to suggest Shakespeare's Coriolanus whose "heart's his mouth," close as the substance of the two speeches may be. Shakespeare, then, as compared with Plutarch, demoralizes his citizens and makes Coriolanus more likeable. Everybody calls Coriolanus proud, but his pride is not a simple matter: much of it, including his unwillingness to boast of his achievements and his horror of exploiting those achievements for his own political ends, belong to humility rather than to pride—for of course we cannot believe that his modesty is an affectation. Again, Coriolanus cannot lie, and a man who cannot lie is irresistibly attractive, however inadequate his hold on truth. This shift of emphasis on Shakespeare's part is clearly a fact of major importance, and we naturally wonder why it has been made.

With a second-rate dramatist, or even with the best dramatists of an ideological age like our own, our first question would be, which side is he on? This is really a question about his general or habitual reactions. Does he, in general, prefer patricians or plebeians? Does he, in general, sympathize with authority or with rebellion? In my own graduate-student days, when fascism was still a world force, we used to talk a good deal about whether the Roman plays showed "fascist tendencies" on Shakespeare's part or not. But of course there is no analogy between fascism and Coriolanus. A fascist leader is a demagogue, and a demagogue is precisely what Coriolanus is not. Further, fascism is a disease of modern democracy, and it is abundantly clear that the society of Coriolanus is pre-democratic.

It is difficult for us, living in an age when politics is so dominated by theory, even to conceive of an imagination so specific and concrete as Shakespeare's. As far as our evidence goes, Shakespeare could hardly have cared less whether in general one should approve of the patrician or the plebeian case. His change of emphasis can have had only one purpose: to make the dramatic conflict as sharp and as evenly balanced as possible. We should remember that the very structure of his drama, with its easy mingling of noblemen and commoners, struck the patricians of his own time as somewhat subversive to begin with. You will recall Sir Henry Wotton's letter about *Henry VIII*, and his complaint that it made greatness too familiar. The mere fact that the citizens are there in *Coriolanus* gives them an initial advantage, and Shakespeare's shift of emphasis indicates his dramatic impartiality. The outcome of the conflict in *Coriolanus* has to seem both tragic and inevitable, and no facile or loaded way of presenting it can accomplish this.

Tragedy is a mixture of the heroic and the ironic. The kind of romance that we have in Malory, where the hero is simply heroic, is one of its boundaries; the kind of ironic situation that we have in *Death of a Salesman*, where the whole point is that the central figure is not a hero, is the other. The admixture of heroism, of a quality which is more than life size, is what makes tragedy, in spite of its sombre and gloomy plot, so profoundly exhilarating. Further, tragedy is independent of morality in the sense that it makes no difference to the structure of tragedy whether its hero is a good man or a bad one. When Macbeth finally understands that he has been cheated of all his hopes by a series of quibbles, and that his fate, so to speak, has gone over to the enemy, he says:

> Yet I will try the last: before my body
> I throw my warlike shield

and we realize that whatever Macbeth has done, he is still a hero, and is worth having a tragedy written about him.

Plutarch tells us that Coriolanus's father died in his infancy and that he was brought up solely by his mother. He adds that Coriolanus married at his mother's request, and continued to live in his mother's house after marriage. For anyone with Shakespeare's insight into human nature, this was all the information he needed for his conception of Coriolanus. There are at least two characters in Shakespeare who suffer from a mother-fixation, Coriolanus and Bertram in *All's Well*. But the person who tries hardest to break Bertram of his mother-fixation is his mother. The Countess of Rousillon is a shrewd and intelligent woman, and these are not adjectives that anyone would apply to the obsessed Volumnia, of whom the tribunes remark, "They say she's mad." There is much in Coriolanus himself that has the charm, as well as the gaucherie, of a boy. The crucial scenes are almost a boy's daydreams come true. He fights with a physical prowess so gigantic that we may wonder what the Romans needed the rest of the army for, and his return is a you'll-be-sorry triumph in which only the pleas of mother and sweetheart can fend off the annihilation of those who have wronged him. In Plutarch Coriolanus fights his way into Corioli with only a handful of followers; in Shakespeare he fights his way in alone. In Plutarch he is banished from Rome with a very few followers; in Shakespeare he goes out alone.

This introversion is a part of a curious immaturity in Coriolanus. Other people are never quite real to him. We remember how he asks mercy for a Volscian prisoner who had befriended him, and then cannot remember his name. It is an exquisite touch, not found in Plutarch, but exquisite touches in Shakespeare are not lugged in; they are there because they belong there. The repetition of the word "voices" emphasizes how ghostly society is to Coriolanus, and why the citizens hate him so. The citizens, however vacillating and misled, are not without their own dignity. "The price is, to ask it kindly"— that is the voice of a human being, not of a rabble. They are used to being pushed around and told that they are not much good, and they will take a good deal from Menenius Agrippa, will allow him to tell them his preposterous fable of the belly and the members, because he at least has his eyes focussed on them when he talks to them. But how do you cope with a man who treats you as though you were a dream in his mind, and an unpleasant dream at that?

It is clear that the sexual energy of Coriolanus has gone into warfare, and that his real mistress is Bellona. This is also true of Tullus Aufidius. As this present production has tried to suggest, Coriolanus and Tullus are enemies, and therefore they are lovers. It seems a curious 'therefore,' but Coriolanus in his own way does love his enemies. For enmity, though it may use the language of hatred, is not hatred, any more than love is lust. The coward is typically the man who can neither fight nor love his enemies: he may hate and despise his enemy, but his instinct, in a crisis, is to do what his enemy wants him to do. It is one of Tullus's servants who makes the terrifying remark, which we have not found the answer to yet, that while war breeds enmity, peace breeds more hatred, because then men have less need of one another. Coriolanus is a man who must have an enemy, and that is why he is able to turn against his own city without, so far as we can see, the slightest twinge of conscience. But the fact that enmity is more essential to him than friendship indicates once again a lack of some element of maturity. When at the end of the play Tullus calls him "boy," Coriolanus breaks down completely. It is, as he says, the first time he was ever forced to scold; it is also the first time that he boasts of his exploits. In many respects the tragedy of Coriolanus is like the tragedy of St. Joan in Shaw, a tragedy founded on inexperience in dealing with other people and on the brutal tactlessness of youth.

Coriolanus, then, is a man without a mask, or fully developed social personality. This word "personality" reminds us of the fact that the "dramatis personae" at the beginning of a play originally meant the masks used in the performance, and psychology still uses the word "persona" to mean the social aspect of character. In Coriolanus there is nothing to mediate between his thought and his expression, or between an outside stimulus and his inner response. His enemies know this, and know in advance how he will react to certain words, such as "traitor"—although, when Tullus Aufidius calls him that, he is a traitor, or at least has put himself in a traitorous position. But the social personality is what enables us to live in a community, and it is especially the function of a leader to create a community. Society disintegrates around Coriolanus: his soldiers will follow him with great enthusiasm as long as things are going well, but at the first check they break apart or fall to looting. Contrast them with the soldiers of Mark Antony, fighting like demons and joking about their wounds, even Enobarbus, who sees through Antony like glass, committing suicide out of shame at deserting him. With a fully-developed personality goes the power that Mark Antony has and that Coriolanus conspicuously lacks—the power of rhetoric. Coriolanus often speaks well and nobly, but he cannot accommodate his speech to a specific occasion or influence human actions by his speech. Even at his best he is imprisoned in his own sense of integrity. One comes away from this production with a great admiration for Mr. Scofield, not simply for the obvious reasons, but for surmounting a difficulty peculiar to this role. Mr. Scofield has to act the part of a man who cannot act a part, whose whole attitude to life is anti-dramatic.

Shakespeare may well have been fascinated by Coriolanus, because he is a figure so antipathetic to Shakespeare himself—Shakespeare who, so far as we know him, is nothing but mask and the power of rhetoric, who never, so far as we know, speaks to us from his heart, and whose nature is subdued to what it works in, like the dyer's hand. Shakespeare must have been profoundly aware of the importance of rhetoric in holding a society together and of the necessity for all the devices of tact, accommodation, even hypocrisy (for "hypocrite" was also originally a metaphor of a masked actor) in saving faces and coddling egos and generally keeping the social machinery running. He was aware too of the importance of the arts in society, especially of those two arts, music and drama, which are ensemble performances for audiences, and manifest more vividly than any other arts the presence of a community. The predominance of music and drama in Elizabethan culture shows its sense of community, just as the predominance of essay and novel in Victorian culture shows its sense of individuality. Coriolanus, though a patrician, is not a conservative: the only soliloquy he makes speaks with contempt of custom and the error it accumulates. Given peacetime power, he would be less like Caesar or Antony than like that other ruthless Puritanical revolutionary, Cassius, and we remember what Caesar says of Cassius to Mark Antony:

> He loves no plays,
> As thou dost, Antony: he hears no music.

It seems most probable that *Coriolanus* preceded *Timon of Athens* and followed *Antony and Cleopatra*. It is usually called the last of the Roman plays, but I should prefer to call it the third of the four Plutarchan plays. Plutarch is a garrulous writer, and his life of Antony contains a digression on the misanthrope Timon. Plutarch's lives are "parallel" lives in which a biography

of a Roman follows that of a Greek whose career resembles or contrasts with his, after which a comparison
between the two is usually made. The Greek parallel
to Coriolanus is Timon's friend, Alcibiades, a contrast in
every way, a born intriguer with no principles except
that of advancing his own interests, yet able to charm
even those who knew that they could not trust him.
Plutarch remarks that Coriolanus, for all his virtues,
could not make himself loved, and that Alcibiades, for
all his vices, could not make himself hated. In *Timon
of Athens*, that extraordinary play (one I hope Stratford
will soon perform), part morality and part folk tale,
which forms the transition between the great tragedies
and the later romances, a theme from *Coriolanus* reappears. Alcibiades is banished from Athens but returns
with an army to compel its surrender. Here there is no
tragedy, only a patching up of differences, for in this
play the tragic emphasis falls on Timon, whose mis-
anthropy makes him so isolated from the action that he
tries to identify himself with everything destructive and
chaotic in nature.

Coriolanus is a victim of his own sincerity, not unlike
Molière's misanthropic Alceste, and it is easy to see
why Shakespeare went from Coriolanus to the misanthrope Timon. In these plays, especially *Coriolanus,* the
tragedy is confined to the human world. Plutarch is
fond of omens and auguries, and in his life of Coriolanus
there are several opportunities for giving a supernatural
dimension to the action. But Shakespeare ignores all
these: he wants no suggestion of the supernatural in
this particular play. In the world which Shakespeare
and his audience shared, there are several levels of

nature. At the bottom is time, the enemy and devourer, time that sweeps all things away into oblivion. Above it is the turning wheel of fortune and the cycle of nature, bringing some regularity into existence but still alien and hostile to human desire. We notice in the sonnets the connection of royal figures with the cycle of nature, the sun rising to its zenith and then falling as

> The eyes, 'fore duteous, now converted are
> From his low tract, and look another way.

The world of the wheel is the order of physical nature, a world man is in but not of, because it has in itself no moral significance. Above it is man's proper world, the world of human nature, a world civilized by law, education, religion and art. Yet even in this world good and evil are together, and love and loyalty cannot be wholly separated from much that is false and hypocritical. The failure to respect the conditions of a world where good and evil are inseparable can lead only to tragedy, even for Coriolanus whose nature is said by Menenius Agrippa to be too noble for this world. In *Coriolanus* a great artificer in words demonstrates, however indirectly and obliquely, the vast power of ordered speech in forming the destinies of mankind, and the disaster that awaits those who, whether from impatient sincerity like Coriolanus, or from outraged idealism like Timon, cannot enter into the kind of social contract that is symbolized by the theatre and its audience.

QUESTIONS FROM THE FLOOR

Q. What do you think of Bernard Shaw's view that *Coriolanus* is Shakespeare's greatest comedy?

A. I am not familiar with the Shaw passage, but my reference to Molière's *Alceste* indicates that the central situation is of a sort that might appear in a comedy, though a very sombre one. The more one disapproves politically of Coriolanus, the more purely ironic, and hence nearer to comedy, his fall will appear to be.

Q. Is not the stress on Coriolanus's homosexual relation to Tullus and his mother-fixation post-Freudian, and consequently both dated for us and anachronistic for Shakespeare?

A. Freud said that he had discovered only what the poets had always known. Coriolanus's relation to his mother is stressed in the text to a degree unusual in Shakespeare: even the crowd says that he fights to please his mother, and he is continually turning to that marmoreal and matronly stupidity with a pathetic desire for approval. He is also twice described in the text as like a "mistress" to Tullus Aufidius. In Shakespeare's great plays the structure of human relations is so complex and so delicately balanced that a performance almost exaggerates an aspect of it simply by trying to bring it out.

Q. Is there not good evidence of at least an aesthetic dislike of the populace on Shakespeare's part? He often speaks of their greasy caps and their stinking breaths.

A. This kind of reaction is appropriate for a poet who deals with sense experience more directly than with concepts. Politically, Shakespeare seems to regard the crowd as largely the creation of its leaders. Without leadership it becomes a many-headed monster, a mob, not a society. And a mob, no matter who the individuals are who compose it, is always subhuman.

Q. Did Shakespeare use *Coriolanus* as a vehicle for commenting on social conditions in his time—shortages of food and the like?

A. I think if Shakespeare had been more interested in social criticism he would have made more use of the material Plutarch could have afforded him. The passage on the money-lenders I mentioned reminds us of the crying abuse of monopolies in Shakespeare's day. The difficulty with topical allusions is that they have to be subtle enough to get past the censor and broad enough to get across to the audience—an almost impossible requirement. Shakespeare's topical allusions seem to be mainly about the weather—obviously he preferred to say only what he could say openly, and his instinct for keeping out of trouble was highly developed. Scholars regret this: the law courts are the best documented part of Elizabethan life, and if Shakespeare had only got into trouble we should know much more about him than we do.

Q. How does Tullus Aufidius compare with Coriolanus?

A. He seems more accessible to jealousy and resentment, but perhaps only because he is in a position to be so. The accuracy with which he places the word "boy," however, indicates an element of cunning in him which makes him a smaller man than Coriolanus.

Q. Is Coriolanus's decision not to attack Rome a sign of submission to his mother or a sign that he has escaped from her domination?

A. It seems to me a gesture of submission, brought out in his despairing cry, "Oh mother, what have you done?" Coriolanus is prepared for the assault on his feelings, and has made up his mind to resist it. What he

doesn't know is that Volumnia is his superior officer, that
he cannot function as a soldier without her direction.

Q. This production dressed the actors in Napoleonic
costume. What kind of modern situation could we imagine Coriolanus in?

A. When the Elizabethans thought of Rome they
usually thought of imperial Rome: Coriolanus of course
belongs to a much earlier time. Plutarch comments on
the primitive barbaric nature of his age, when the words
for virtue and military valour were the same. As an
historical figure Coriolanus hardly belongs to an age
like that of Napoleon, who according to Shaw was the
man who discovered that if a cannon ball hit a man it
would kill him. That is, he has no impersonal or logistic
conception of warfare: he fights with his own hands.
Similarly, no modern democracy would elect Coriolanus
to be dog-catcher; but Coriolanus could not exist in a
modern democracy. There is perhaps something of the
Victorian dowager about Volumnia: one could imagine
her sending Coriolanus out from Eton to govern India
and assume the white man's burden. Even so, an historical situation like that of Coriolanus would have to
be an isolated or frontier situation. But of course the
human situation which the historical one symbolizes is
independent of historical setting.

Q. Would you comment on the relation of Menenius
Agrippa to Coriolanus?

A. I suppose Menenius Agrippa is the only father
Coriolanus has, and he certainly has himself a strongly
paternal feeling for Coriolanus. Falstaff similarly has a
paternal feeling for Prince Henry, and the dismissal of
Menenius Agrippa is like a smaller version of the rejec-

tion of Falstaff, a young man casting off an older one in a way which is not simply a snub but destroys the older man's self-respect and his whole reason for living.

Q. Is Coriolanus portrayed as emotional enough to give credibility to his relation to his mother and to Tullus Aufidius?

A. His emotions are not outgoing ones. What one admires about Mr. Scofield's rendering of the part is its restraint, the sense of a tremendous smoldering power that never quite breaks through. If it did break through, he would no longer be Coriolanus, but someone more like Mark Antony or Othello.

Peter Dwyer was born in England and educated at Dulwich College and Keble College, Oxford. His first work was connected with theatre and film in Oxford, London, and Paris, but since 1940 he has worked primarily for the British or Canadian governments. He was first a member of the British Foreign Service, then a member of the Cabinet Secretariat in the Office of the Privy Council, and, since 1958, he has been Supervisor of the Arts Programme of the Canada Council.

PETER DWYER

William Shakespeare's first performance:

AN ENTERTAINMENT FOR SPECULATORS

(Mr. Dwyer opened his talk with an amusing anecdote
designed to illustrate among other things that he was
not a professional scholar. This printed version of his
manuscript starts at the point where he began to develop his main argument.—Editor)

I think it possible that I may be able to re-examine
usefully for you an aspect of Shakespeare's boyhood
which was first brought to light in a footnote to an
obscure work by Canon Raine in 1837 and to which
some attention is paid in *The Annotator* by **Alan Keen**
and Roger Lubbock. Or perhaps, I should rather say
that I will put together certain pieces of evidence which
are common knowledge in a way that has not so far
been done in any detail. This permits me to draw the
very tentative conclusion that Shakespeare as a boy
had a little act or "party-piece" which he would perform to amuse his friends; that he showed, as Sir Edmund Chambers suggests briefly, "some early exercise
of mimic talent."

In the end you may perhaps not agree with me. But
I do think that as a by-product of what I have to say I
can supply you with a correct interpretation of a line

in *Hamlet* which really has escaped the attention of editors. And indeed, I shall later have to use this line to prop up my arguments.

Before I present the evidence to you, I must first explain exactly what I mean by a "party-piece." When I was a boy, some 35 years ago now, it was the custom for there to be some entertainment in the home after family friends had come to supper. By about seven o'clock the veal loaf so carefully turned out of the blanc-mange shape, in which it was made, to tremble in its jelly like a vast bosom unlikely sprouted in the middle of the table, had gone the way all bosoms, alas, must go; the potato salad, a recipe from Aunt Carrie which called for *real* cream, had become a faint smear in the dish; the trifle—just a touch of rum which couldn't possibly do you any harm—had been reduced to a yellow shambles. Then we would all move to the drawing-room and the piano would be opened — a Broadwood like Beethoven had once — and the "party-pieces" would begin.

Aunt Edith, riding high in her corsets and on the rum in the trifle, and virgin to her shuddering core, would sing with a voice like a sharp skewer "Softly awakes my heart" from Saint-Saens' *Samson and Delilah*—an aria of dark seduction, but French and therefore somehow excusable. And then Uncle Eric, almost totally circum-scribed by a gold watch chain and smelling of beer wisely taken before arrival, who rose late every morning and hoped never to set foot outside greater London if he could help it, would render "Heigh ho, come to the Fair, with maidens and men in the pride of the morn-ing." And at last a small boy would recite Lord Byron's

"The Destruction of Sennacherib," his face distorted
with an agony caused equally by apprehension of his
audience and a desire to go to the lavatory before the
last verse.

This was the party-piece, then. It had had a long and
honourable career in the English-speaking world rising
to its height, perhaps, under Victoria. We find plenty
of examples of it in Pepys' diary, and it represents as it
were the nod of the middle classes towards the performing arts. It is, of course, very easy to make fun of
party-pieces, but we must now take them a little more
seriously. They represented, I think, the last survival of
a time when the arts were a more natural expression of
a man and when the virtuosity of the professional had
not yet shamed us all out of our innate desire to perform. Often they represented hours of practice and
loving care exercised in private, and the persons who
brought them to the uncertain point of public performance are perhaps more to be admired than the
thumbsuckers of the television screen.

Now, if I am to persuade you that Shakespeare as a
boy might have had just such a party-piece, I must
first try to establish that a little act or party-piece was
available to him when he was living in his father's house
in Stratford. Then later on I will try to link this act to
Shakespeare himself. To suggest the possibility that
such an act was available I have first a group of three
items of documentation to present to you. They range
over a period of four centuries.

The first is taken from the Revels Account for Princess Mary at Christmastide 1521. I quote it as it appears
in Miss H. F. M. Prescott's biography of Mary I: "Item

pd. to a man at Wyndesore, for killing a calffe before my ladys grace behynde a clothe." For the second item we now jump forward some 250 years to a notice which appeared in the *Newcastle Chronicle* on December 22nd, 1775, as quoted by Canon Raine in a glossary note in the *Priory of Finchale,* Surtees Society, 1837: "Lately died at Barnard Castle, Joney Davie, alias Davidson, aged 95, well known to most people in the county of Durham, in being noted for begging about, and getting his living by a droll performance which he called killing the calf." "The son of this man, a second Joney Davie (Canon Raine adds), was a dancing master and he too killed a calf." The third item, which is something of a makeweight but nonetheless interesting is taken from the novel, *Mountolive,* by Lawrence Durrell, first published in 1958: "It was late when we walked back together towards Trafalgar Square in the falling snow. There were few people about and the snowflakes deadened our footsteps. In the Square itself your poet stopped to apostrophize Nelson Stylites in true calf-killing fashion. I have forgotten exactly what he said, but it was sufficiently funny to make me laugh very heartily."

Now let us for a moment consider the significance of these items one by one and in a juxtaposition in which I have placed them. At the time of the entry in the household accounts made in 1521, Mary was a little girl some five years old. Miss Prescott in her biography consequently refers to the killing of a calf as "a mysterious and gruesome performance," and it seems hardly suitable for a child's entertainment if it is taken to mean literally what it says. But if the phrase "killing of a calffe" is considered in the light of the extract from the *Newcastle Chronicle* we then have the possibility that it was in fact a comic act, quite suitable for a young child, which had endured in the performance of clowns for some 250 years.

Although I cannot produce any evidence to provide certainty, I myself find it quite reasonable to suppose that these two items refer to one and the same thing. I do not think it at all surprising that a good comic turn should endure for over two centuries—for traditions in the theatre are durable and theatre people are often surprisingly conservative. I can give a fairly simple example of the durability of Shakespearian tradition in the theatre. During rehearsals for a performance of *A Midsummer Night's Dream* in which I took part some years ago, the producer instructed the actor playing Bottom to fall on his sword in the clowns' play in such a way that Thisbe would not be able to find it subsequently and so that she would eventually be forced to stab herself with the scabbard. The producer did not pretend that this was an original idea. He said: "They always do it." This piece of business must, I think, have survived from the first performance of the play by Shakespeare's own company; because in Edward Sharpham's play, *The Fleir*, published in 1607, we find this reference: "Faith, like Thisbe in the play, 'a has almost kil'd himselfe with the scabbard." So here is a piece of stage business surviving some 350 years and crossing the ocean intact.

Then we should, I think, note that the elder Joney Davie had apparently handed on the act to his son, the dancing master. It is therefore not illogical to assume that the father himself may have been taught the act in his youth. There is at least a slight indication here of a tradition. We should also note that in 1775 the elder Davie was 95 years old and had consequently been born in 1680. It is worth remembering this date because, as we shall see when I present some further evidence to you, there were at that time actors still alive who had survived the closing of the theatres in 1642 and were a living link with the Jacobean theatre.

I hope that I may therefore have persuaded you that there is a strong possibility that the "Killing of a calf" was a clown's act already in existence at the beginning of the sixteenth century and still going strong at the end of the eighteenth. We must therefore consider what kind of an act it may have been; but from the works of reference available to me I have not been able to find any contemporary description of it.

On the evidence before us we can only say that it appears to have been a show that could be performed, indeed was performed, by a single actor. There must have been some properties used because some representation of a calf, or perhaps a calf's head, would surely have been required. In the sixteenth century a cloth of some kind was also used. I have been in correspondence with Miss Prescott who has subsequently agreed that the performance was not "mysterious or gruesome" but was almost certainly the same as that referred to as the droll performance of Joney Davie. The mention of the cloth made her wonder if perhaps the act might have been a sort of shadow play—the best of this kind are but shadows—but here we have no evidence, and so far can only speculate.

Nor do word meanings seem to serve us. We can find a usage of "Kill" in 1375 meaning simply to "strike, to hit, or to beat," but there has been no evidence that I can find of a later survival of this limited meaning. "Calf" is quite commonly used in the seventeenth century to mean "a fool" as in Drayton's line "Some silly doting brainless calf." A combination of these two meanings might give us the sense of "beating the fool," but I can find no authority for this interpretation and I do not think it in any way persuasive. There is a reference in 1630 to "Kill-calf cruelty and sheep-slaughtering murder," but this seems to me to be an image drawn directly from butchery.

Sir Edmund Chambers, on whom I would lean in these matters as on the rock of ages, says: "Killing a calf *seems* to have been an item in the repertory of wandering entertainers." The authors of *The Annotator*, Alan Keen and Roger Lubbock, are much more specific. "The performance of Killing the Calf (they say) was merely a comedy 'turn.' A clown would indulge in crosstalk with a dummy head pushed through the curtain. When the calf's head became too glib for the interrogator, the clown seized a broadsword of wood and struck off the head, which tumbled onto the stage." However, in providing this description they give no sources for their information and in referring to Canon Raine they spell his name incorrectly. They are therefore gentlemen in whom I do not have an absolute trust. However, it is possible that they are right. Though when Sir Edmund Chambers says "seems," we must have some doubts about scholars who say (as it were): "Seems . . . ? Nay, it is: I know not seemes . . ."

We come finally, however, to what does appear to be a reliable description as far as it goes. Commenting on the quotation in the *Newcastle Chronicle*, Canon Raine has this to say: "There was an old dramatic representation called Killing the Calf. The performer played his part behind a door or curtain, and, by means of ventriloquism, acted at once the butcher and the animal. The one talked and pitied; the other moaned and seemed to pray for mercy, till its moving solicitations became fainter and fainter, and it appeared to die." Although the Canon gives no source he seems to write with authority and relates (though he does not quote it) the entry in the accounts of Princess Mary.

There remains the phrase from Lawrence Durrell's *Mountolive* — "In true calf-killing fashion" — and this seems to me in the context to be used in the sense we are searching after. Mountolive is recalling the aftermath of a dinner party he had with the poet, Pursewarden, and his sister where they became rather gay over the wine. There is a clear suggestion in the passage of histrionics. I have arranged for a friend to ask Mr. Durrell what the phrase means to him, but unfortunately there has not yet been time for a reply. Nevertheless, whatever it may have been, a comic act performed by one person certainly seems to have existed. The question now is whether or not there is any reason to suppose that Shakespeare himself was familiar with this act and might perhaps have performed it as a young lad in Stratford. I should like to suggest very tentatively —and indeed in this company with considerable humility—that such a possibility does exist.

I have two further pieces of evidence to present for

your consideration. The first will be well known to you
and is taken from the *Brief Lives* of John Aubrey, writing in about 1681, and believed to have visited Stratford
in the 1660's: "His father was a butcher, and I have
been told theretofore by some of the neighbours, that
when he was a boy he exercised his father's trade, but
when he killed a calfe, he would do it in a high style
and make a speech." The second item is from *Hamlet*,
Act III, Scene 2, from the preamble to the play within
the play:

POLONIUS: I did enact Julius Caesar, I was kill'd i' th'
Capitol: Brutus kill'd me.

HAMLET: It was a bruite part of him, to kill so Capi-
tall a calfe there. Be the players ready?

Now if you would keep the quotation from Aubrey
in the back of your minds for a moment, I should like
first to consider these lines from *Hamlet*. Polonius, as
you will remember, is reminiscing about his days of
amateur acting at the University while waiting for the
play to begin, having perhaps in the back of his mind
the thought that if he were put to it he might still be
able to give as good a performance as the actors he is
about to see. Hamlet clearly has little or no opinion of
Polonius as an actor, and with a dreary quibble on
"Brute" and "Brutus" draws an analogy between Polonius' performance of Caesar and the Killing of a Calf.

Yet no editor that I have been able to discover in-
terprets Hamlet's remark in the light of the evidence I
have put before you. Passing perhaps with a shudder
over the Brutus pun, they leave the line without a
comment—attributing no doubt the rest of the remark to

the wild and whirling words of Hamlet's feigned madness. But surely Hamlet's remark only has point and
sting when it is understood to imply that Polonius' performance as Julius Caesar was no better than a comic
act by a clown. In other words, there was method in
Hamlet's madness in this remark as elsewhere in the
play. I have already demonstrated to you the strong
possibility that this clown's act must have been in
existence during Shakespeare's lifetime, and if it was
fairly popular at the time the meaning of Hamlet's sneer
would not escape the audience. I personally have little
doubt that in this line Shakespeare is referring to the
act which was performed before Princess Mary in 1521
and which was part of Joney Davie's stock in trade in
the late eighteenth century. This suggestion is also
made by Alan Keen in *The Annotator*. If you will agree
that this may well be so, we now come to the heart of
the matter, and must consider whether or not Shakespeare might himself have performed this act as a
party-piece when he was a boy. For there seems to be
little doubt that Shakespeare knew about the act.

The next stage of this investigation then must be to
establish whether John Aubrey, writing that Shakespeare as a boy killed a calf, meant the phrase to be
taken literally or whether he too was referring to the
clown's act which we have been discussing. I think that
in the context and with the reference to Shakespeare's
father being a butcher, there can be little doubt that
Aubrey meant his statement to be taken at face value,
that he meant quite literally that young Shakespeare
would make a speech when he butchered a calf for his
father.

If this is so, we must then consider whether there exists any possibility that Aubrey could have misunderstood what was told him by one of his sources, that he might have taken literally and wrongly a phrase which was in fact theatre jargon with which he was not familiar. This possibility which is central to my theme needs to be examined very carefully. And I must warn you that in doing so, I shall be forced to speculate rather more than I have done so far.

Aubrey had been collecting for an Oxford archaeologist called Anthony Wood a mass of biographical material on his contemporaries and their immediate forbears. Although he was an archaeologist himself and a Fellow of the Royal Society, Aubrey's chief qualifications as a biographer were perhaps an intense curiosity, an eagerness on every occasion to believe the worst of his subject, and an inimitable style. His sources of information were frequently very good indeed, but reading him leaves, I feel, a strong impression that he does not always distinguish between fact and fiction. Here is a splendid example of Aubrey at work: "Ben Johnson had one eie lower than t'other, and bigger, like Clun, the player: perhaps he begott Clun." Again he can draw a beautiful thumbnail sketch as in his description of Gwynn, the Earl of Oxford's secretary: "A better instance of a squeamish and disobliging, slighting, insolent, proud fellow, perhaps can't be found than in Gwin, the earl of Oxford's secretary. No reason satisfies him, but he overweenes, and cuts some sower faces that would turne the milk in a faire ladie's breast." Here is Aubrey on Edmund Waller, the poet who wrote that most beautiful line of three words, "Go, lovely rose":

"He haz but a tender weake body but was alwayes very temperate. One . . . made him damnable drunke at Somerset-house, where, at the water-stayres, he fell down, and had a cruel fall. 'Twas pitty to use such a sweet swan so inhumanely." Lively, informed, charming, and not always entirely accurate.

Now Shakespeare's father was not a butcher. He is referred to in contemporary legal documents as a glover or whittawer, and of this trade there can be no doubt. So Aubrey is wrong in his statement, and it seems quite possible to me that he drew this conclusion because he had been told that Will Shakespeare killed a calf in a high style. In the sixteenth century a glover could not also have been a butcher, for the Tanner's Act specifically forbade all tanners of leather to have anything to do with the sale of meat. Of course John Shakespeare did have other interests and he may at times have done some butchering. But it was nevertheless incorrect to describe him flatly as a butcher.

However, before we consider if Aubrey was in touch with any source close to the theatre who might have used the phrase "killing a calf" in its theatre sense, we must first deal with the possibility that young Shakespeare worked as a butcher for someone other than his father.

There is some evidence to support this possibility. John Dowdall who visited Warwickshire in 1693 and enquired into some facts of Shakespeare's life in Stratford states that the old sexton of the church told him that Shakespeare "was formerly in this town bound apprentice to a butcher"; and this seems to give at least some support to what Aubrey had to say. In his *Life of*

William Shakespeare Joseph Quincey Adams suggests
that the butcher might well have been William Tyler
of Sheep Street who was for some considerable time
closely associated with John Shakespeare in municipal
affairs. In his will Shakespeare made the following entry in the first draft: "Item 1 give and bequeath to Mr.
Richard Tyler the elder XXVIs VIIId to buy him a
ring." This Richard was the son of William Tyler, and
consequently the entry argues some friendship between
the Shakespeare and Tyler families. This is, of course,
speculation, but I think we must admit that there is
some evidence (or at least a tradition in Stratford at the
end of the seventeenth century) that Shakespeare may
have worked for a time as a butcher's apprentice—
though this butcher was almost certainly not his father.

But even if this was so, it does not altogether exclude
the possibility that Shakespeare's "killing of the calf"
was a comic act. Indeed if he had worked in a butcher's
shop the act might have had a particular appeal to him
if perhaps he first saw it done by one of the players
from the companies that visited Stratford when he was
a boy. Aubrey says that he had the story of Shakespeare
killing the calf from some of the neighbours—and perhaps he did. But what seems to me of particular importance are a number of entries jotted down in Aubrey's manuscript notes. The first reads: "W. Shakespeare
—q(uaere) Mr. Beeston, who knows most of him . . ."
And then in a second note: "Did I tell you that I have
mett with old Mr. (Beeston), who knew all the old
English poets, whose lives I am taking from him?" And,
noting down that Beeston told him that Shakespeare

understood Latin fairly well, he wrote in the margin opposite: "from Mr. Beeston."

Now: William Beeston was an old theatre manager who had survived the closing of the theatres and lived on into the Restoration. Dryden called him "the chronicle of the stage." And what is even more important is that William Beeston was the son of Christopher Beeston who was a member of the company of actors which Shakespeare joined when he first came to London. He is listed as a member of the Lord Chamberlain's company and as a performer in Ben Jonson's *Every Man in his Humour* in the edition published in 1598. Shakespeare was also in this production. In 1617 Christopher Beeston built the Cockpit Playhouse in Drury Lane and his son William was associated with him in the management of the theatre for many years. So here we have John Aubrey, who wrote about Shakespeare killing the calf, sitting down for a long talk with an old theatre man, who was garrulous enough to be called the chronicle of the stage, and who was the son of one of Shakespeare's colleagues. And if all Aubrey's intense curiosity brought out during their chat was that Shakespeare was quite good at Latin and worked for a time as a schoolmaster, then he was not the man I take him to be. Nor do I believe that an old actor, given half a chance to talk about the great days, would not have rambled on with stories and anecdotes about the theatre and theatre people. And since the very subject of Aubrey's enquiry was William Shakespeare, should we not reasonably expect old William Beeston to have drawn on theatre gossip which he must have had from his father in the old days?

I warned you that I should speculate, and now I am
going to do so on an even larger scale. I think it is entirely possible that it was William Beeston who might
have mentioned the killing of the calf. Actors, like all
professional people, are apt to use the jargon of their
trade with the assumption that their interlocutor will
understand at once what they mean. If William Beeston
recounted a story that his father had told him of how
Shakespeare used to perform a comic act when he was a
boy in Stratford, it might well be that it would never
occur to him that he should explain to Aubrey what he
meant by "killing the calf." It would not be inconsistent
with Aubrey's character for him to have kept this piece
of information in the back of his mind, to have misunderstood the terminology, and to have related it to
what he may have learned in Stratford about Shakespeare's apprenticeship to a butcher. And even if he did
not have the story from old Beeston, it is still possible
that Aubrey could have misconstrued what he was told
by someone else.

I feel that on the whole this suggestion is more acceptable than the statement that when he butchered a calf
young Shakespeare did it in a high style and made a
speech. This statement seems to me not to ring true.
For it is surely certain that in a brutal age Shakespeare
was unusually sensitive to the suffering of animals. It is
possible to demonstrate with some certainty this characteristic of Shakespeare's by drawing upon Caroline
Spurgeon's *Shakespeare's Imagery*. Here is Miss Spurgeon's conclusion: "Shakespeare's attitude as seen in
his images is unique among the dramatists of his time,
for he shows a sympathy with and understanding of the

animal's point of view and sufferings which no one else in his age approaches." Alone among writers of the time, he thinks of the hunted or snared animal, with the poor bird "fearing the net and lime, the pitfall and the gin, of the falcon mewed up, and of the bear tied to the stake." Miss Spurgeon points out that in his hunting images we are conscious "not of the joyous abandon of the sportsman, but of the 'fell and cruel hounds' pursuing the 'moody-mad and desperate' stag, 'hunted even to falling.' So much is this the case, that out of thirty-nine hunting images, I only once find the hunt pictured as a gay and joyous pastime, . . ."

It would be possible to give many examples of Shakespeare's sensitivity to the suffering of animals, but from our point of view perhaps the most significant images are those which Miss Spurgeon draws mainly from Parts 2 and 3 *Henry VI* and which seem to show a particular distaste for the slaughterhouse. Henry sees "Duke Humphrey as a calf taken away by the butcher, bound, beaten and borne to the bloody slaughter-house, while he, Henry,

As the dam runs lowing up and down,
Looking the way her harmless young one went."

In Part 3 *Henry VI* (Miss Spurgeon says) "Clifford, Edward and Clarence are called 'butchers,' Richard is 'that devil's butcher,' parliament is thought of as a 'shambles,' and the realm as a 'slaughter-house,' Gloucester sees himself hewing his way to the crown with a bloody axe, and Henry, when Gloucester comes to kill him, pictures himself very aptly as a sheep yielding his throat unto the butcher's knife."

Through the spy-glass which Miss Spurgeon holds out to us we see something of Shakespeare's sub-conscious mind, and we observe a man who for his time must have been abnormally sensitive to the suffering of animals and who writes of the butcher with obvious distaste. If this was the man, is it then likely that the boy, even if he had to butcher a calf, would have done it in a high style and made a speech? I think not. Of all the things that Aubrey wrote or noted about Shakespeare, this to me rings most untrue. And I therefore suggest that Shakespeare's attitudes revealed in his images tend to support my suggestion that the reference to the killing of a calf is more likely to have been to a clown's act, to a droll performance.

Canon Raine is of the same opinion: "Was this the calf which Shakespeare killed?" he asks, "and was his mighty mind first excited by his popular performance of this antient representation? Did the applause which, in his boyhood, he received at Stratford, when he killed his calf *in high style,* lead to the expanding of his genius, and to that immortal name which he obtained?" I think that the answer to the Canon's questions is: Yes.

I have already speculated, as I warned you I should, and I now propose to end by a short flight of fancy, bred perhaps more in the heart than in the head. I *like* to think that from time to time the Shakespeares had friends in to dinner—perhaps on a summer's afternoon —when Will Shakespeare was a boy. If we again rely on Miss Spurgeon's investigations, I think there would have been some baking early in the morning, and some crisp fresh loaves set out to cool—for Shakespeare particularly disliked doughy ill-baked bread. Since we imagine it was in summer, young William might have been sent out to gather some stuff for fresh salad to be garnished with herbs. I *like* to think that there was honey on the table. The main dish might perhaps have been a sweet goose or, since this was going to be a festive occasion, a good round of beef bought from the Tylers—and care would be taken to make sure that it was not over-roasted. Perhaps there would have been some special sauce because "to make our appetites more keen, with eager compounds we our palate urge." I imagine there would have been cakes, and of course ale to drink.

I *like* to think that the Tylers were invited and that young Richard Tyler, whom Shakespeare was later to remember in the first draft of his will, was there. This would surely have made certain that the beef was a good cut. I like to think that the Shakespeares' neighbours, the Fields, were there. Their son Richard, who was a couple of years older than William, was shortly to go to London to be apprenticed to a printer and was no doubt a little condescending and bursting with reflected glory. Some years later he was to print (and very nicely, too) William's *Venus and Adonis*, and has consequently basked in reflected glory ever since. I *like* to think that the Quineys were also invited and that their boy Richard was there. This was the Richard who in later years was to attempt to borrow some money in London from his loving countryman William Shakespeare who had by then made quite a bit of money in the theatre. And Richard Quiney's son, Thomas, would in later years marry Shakespeare's daughter, Judith. Perhaps (unless I am making Mary Shakespeare's table too large) the Sadlers were also there with their son, Ham-

net or Hamlet, who was later to stand godfather for
Shakespeare's only son, Hamnet. I *like* to think that
these families might have been found all together on
some festive occasion under the Shakespeares' roof—
and from evidence which we have of family relations I
do not think it entirely impossible.

The young people would have included three
Richards (Tyler, Field and Quiney) and William and a
Hamnet. I wonder which of the Richards would have
been called Richard the Third who had died on the field
of Bosworth only some 90 years before? Anyway, I like
to think of the fathers sitting around the table after
dinner, discussing municipal affairs, because at least
three of them, including John Shakespeare, had held
important offices. The ladies presumably might have
been supervising the proper disposal of the dishes and
knives and spoons. I always treasure in the back of my
mind a brief statement written by a harassed lady in the
fourteenth century, and quoted by Arthur Bryant in his
anthology *Postman's Horn,* which says simply: "Sarvints
yis not what they was." I suspect this was as true in
Elizabethan Stratford as it was in the fourteenth century and is still today.

I like to think that meanwhile in the parlour behind
closed doors a surprise was being prepared by the boys.
A sheet perhaps from Mary Shakespeare's best bed was
being tied with cord at two corners and hung pre-
cariously from the beams. Chairs and benches were
being moved about and set out in some order in front
of the cloth. Richard Field, a little older than the others,
was no doubt explaining that the lower corners of the
sheet would have to be held so that the cloth would

hang straight, and I dare say the other two Richards were being organized to do this properly. In the other part of the room young William Shakespeare would be dressing up in some old clothes from the chest in the attic with some assistance from Hamnet. Perhaps an artificial calf's head was brought out of its hiding place where William had hidden it after making it from old pieces of leather left over from his father's trade—for I think he must have been quite good with his hands.

Then when all these preparations were made the parents would be brought in and seated, and young William would launch into his version of the "Killing of the Calf," which perhaps he had first seen that very year done by one of the clowns from the Earl of Leicester's company or the Earl of Worcester's company, both of which visited Stratford two or three times during the 1570's. And I like to imagine that Mary Shakespeare might have been torn between pride at her son's performance and some apprehension that his talent might lead him to associate a little too closely with players and similar undesirable characters.

But most of all I like to imagine that people strolling along Henley Street that afternoon would look up with some surprise and then smile to themselves at the gusts of laughter floating out from the Shakespeares' open windows into the street. Because if what I have suggested to you has any substance at all, then this was the laughter that was to endure for centuries and that you will hear tonight when you see *Love's Labour's Lost* in this very theatre here in Stratford, Ontario.

R. B. PARKER

R. B. Parker is a graduate of the Universities of Liverpool and Birmingham, where he studied at the Shakespeare Institute. After coming to North America as a Fulbright Fellow he taught at the Universities of Texas, Wisconsin, and Colorado before going to the University of Toronto where he is now a member of the Department of English of Trinity College. He has written on a variety of subjects from the Jacobean Theatre (in *Stratford-upon-Avon Studies*) to the contemporary novel and is at present preparing an edition of Greene's *A Quip for an Upstart Courtier* for publication in the Clarendon edition of Greene's *Works*.

R. B. PARKER

Old books and

Elizabethan printing [*]

In this talk I want to do two things: firstly, and quite briefly, to tell those of you who have not yet seen it, what the Sidney Fisher Collection comprises, and what you might particularly look out for when you examine it; secondly, and a little more fully, to talk about the Elizabethan printing practices which produced such books, and the problems which these practices pose for editors, and consequently for interpreters, of Shakespeare's text.

I

As the *Stratford Festival Brochure* informs us, this fine collection of rare books has been loaned to the Festival by Mr. Sidney T. Fisher of Montreal. The result of 15 years' discrimination and patience, it can proudly claim to be one of the most important private collections of Shakespeare books in North America, and indeed in the world.

You will find that the brochure analyzes the exhibit into four main divisions:

*Some illustrative material has been added to this half-hour introduction to the Sidney Fisher rare book collection, but otherwise the talk is substantially as delivered. See the photographs following page 96.

1) *Editions of Shakespeare's own works.* Although there are no examples in the exhibition of the earlier quarto editions of single plays by Shakespeare, Mr. Fisher is the fortunate possessor of a copy of the first collected edition of the plays, edited by Shakespeare's fellow actors, Heminge and Condell, and printed by Jaggard: the great Folio of 1623. This is the most valuable book of the collection, and the most interesting for Shakespeare enthusiasts; without it we should lack texts for eighteen of Shakespeare's plays, besides having only corrupt and inaccurate texts for several more. There are also copies of the next three folios (1632, 1664, 1685), placed together with the first Folio in the centre case. The 1664 Folio is the first to include *Pericles* (printed previously in quarto, but not included by Heminge and Condell); though it also prints as Shakespeare's several plays manifestly not by him: the so-called "Shakespeare Apocrypha." There are some interesting eighteenth-century editions, including important ones by Nicholas Rowe (1709) and Lewis Theobald (1733)—"piddling Theobald," Pope unkindly called him, for his painstaking attention to detail—and such modern labours of love as the beautifully tooled and decorated editions of William Morris and Eric Gill.

2) *Source Books.* Mr. Fisher seems to have at least one copy, and in many cases several copies, of almost every book any scholar has ever suggested as a Shakespeare source. You might notice in particular the source books for the three plays now in production. In *Henry VIII*, Shakespeare used his much-consulted *Chronicles of England, Scotland, and Ireland* by Raphael Holinshed, Edward Halle's *The Union of the Two Illustre*

Families of Lancastre and York, and Foxe's *Book of Martyrs;* Foxe is particularly fascinating: his naïvely horrific woodcuts, so rigid in their agonies, and his scream-by-scream accounts of torture and execution, deprived the essayist, Charles Lamb, of many nights' sleep as a child. Like Mr. Pickwick's fat boy, he is "out to make your flesh creep!" North's translation of Amyot's French translation of Plutarch's *Lives* was Shakespeare's source for *Coriolanus;* you will find first editions of the Greek, French, and English texts cheek by jowl in the exhibition, all open at the life of Coriolanus. No specific source has been found for *Love's Labour's Lost,* but both Lyly's *Euphues* and Florio's *World of Words* have been suggested as targets for the play's satire on affected language. In addition, there are: Castiglione—Belle-forest—Ariosto—Cinthio—Boccaccio—Fabyan—Froissart —Lydgate—Montaigne . . . the line seems to stretch out to the crack of doom, far too long for me to comment on. But do look at the beautifully printed editions in Greek and Latin put out by the Aldine press of Venice about 1500; and notice the variant readings of the two Bibles in the exhibition (both consulted by Shakespeare)—the Church of England's "Bishop's Bible" and Coverdale's more puritanically inclined "Geneva" or "Breeches Bible," so called because it translates Genesis 3:7 as:

". . . they sewed figtree leaves together and made themselves breeches."

3) *Allusion Books.* This section contains books which referred to Shakespeare, either during his own lifetime or within a hundred years of his death. Again the list is

too long to read out in full; but of particular interest are references to Shakespeare by Jonson, Spencer, Burton, Milton, and Dryden—writers fascinating in their own right, quite apart from their homage to Shakespeare. Note, especially, Ben Jonson's poem about the burning down of the Globe theatre during a performance of *Henry VIII*, and Sir Henry Wotton's famous letter recounting details of the event:

> ". . . This was the fatal period of that virtuous fabric, wherein yet nothing did perish but wood and straw, and a few forsaken cloaks; only one man had his breeches set on fire, that would perhaps have broiled him, if he had not by the benefit of a provident wit put it out with bottle ale."

Figtree leaves are, of course, very inflammable!

4) Lastly, the brochure mentions a kind of catch-all category "illustrating incidents of the plays, and of the life, manners and thought of Shakespearean England." This section comprises such things as the Beaumont and Fletcher Folio; other folios printed by Jaggard—including two rival books on heraldry, elaborately printed and coloured; herbals; ancient maps of London and Warwickshire; histories; and books of travel such as Fynes Moryson's *Itinerary* or Tom Coryat's *Crudities*. (Coryat's title shows as much truth as humility!)

Yet these four divisions do not exhaust the riches of the collection. There are items which burst even the fourth category: first editions of settings of Shakespearean songs by Arne and Schubert; early editions of Chaucer, Milton, Walton, Dryden, and Dr. Johnson; first editions of famous critical works on Shakespeare by Hales, Maurice Morgann, Theobald, Elizabeth

Montagu, Farmer, Malone, Oscar Wilde; and, finally, a
gorgeous gallery of gallant photostats — portraits of
Elizabethan worthies, whiskered, be-feathered and
ruffed; replicas of Shakespeare's handwriting and the
manuscript of *Sir Thomas More;* and items of such
oblique interest as Robert Greene's attack on Shakespeare as an "upstart crow beautified with other men's
feathers," or Banks' famous performing horse referred
to by Moth in *Love's Labour's Lost*:

> "And how easy it is to put years to the word 'three,'
> and study three years in two words, the dancing
> horse will tell you." (I:ii:54-7)

—a joke now blunted for modern audiences.

Altogether, it is a most extraordinary collection —
"great riches in a little room"; which Mr. Fisher is very
generous indeed to loan to the Festival.[1] I'm afraid that
if I were the owner, I would be tempted to lock myself
and my documents in a cell and just GLOAT! Like
Patience on a . . .muniment?

II

Apart from their antiquarian charm and value, however, what use are such "old books" to the critic of
Shakespeare? One good answer is quite short, and quite
emphatic: If we did not have such original editions to
consult, we could not obtain good texts of the Shakespeare plays themselves—texts, that is, which faithfully
record what Shakespeare actually wrote.

This concern to get back to what the author himself
originally intended is, curiously enough, of fairly recent

[1] For a full list of books in the Stratford Exhibit, see appendix, pp. 97 ff.

origin. When one calls a writer the "greatest poet in the world," it is surely simple logic to listen to what he has to say? Yet it was the practice of early editors to base each new edition on the edition immediately before it, adopting most of the previous editors' emendations and adding a few more of their own: if they didn't like a phrase, thought it "low" or couldn't understand it, they were quite prepared to cut it out or rewrite it. Instead of Shakespeare — "the greatest poet in the world," as they all invariably claimed—they gave us themselves! Producers tended to be even more drastic, and from the early tinkerings of Davenant, just after the Restoration, to virtual rewritings by such nineteenth-century actor-managers as Irving and Beerbohm Tree, Shakespeare's text was rarely—perhaps never—presented "straight." Interpretation reached such an extreme that the French could applaud a *Hamlet* which ended happily, with Hamlet married to Ophelia!

These liberties were at first supported by an assertion that the Elizabethans were uncouth and *needed* editing; and then, once Shakespeare-worship had set in with the nineteenth century, by a plea that Elizabethan printing was so careless that the original editions were quite unreliable anyway. Only within the twentieth century has there been a strong movement back to the originals. In the theatre, pioneering by such men as Robert Poel and Granville-Barker has resulted in a new respect for the text of Shakespeare and a simplicity of staging which allows that text its full dramatic value; in scholarship, McKerrow, Pollard, Greg, Dover Wilson, and Fredson Bowers have evolved a technique by which the whole printing history of a text may be reconstructed and the author's own wording thus disentangled, with considerable accuracy, from accidental distortions and sophistications. Not to be aware of such scholarship, nay, to boast of one's ignorance, as some benighted critics are still inclined to do, is rather like the *publican* crying out, "Thank you, Lord, that I am not as other men!"

III

The skills of paleography and bibliography are obviously too complicated for me to do more than scratch the surface of them in half an hour, but I think enough can be said to let you see the Fisher collection as something more than merely a collection of "old books."

In the first place, there is the variety in size to consider. The size of a book depends on two things: the size of the original sheet of paper with which the printer begins; and, secondly, the number of times that sheet is folded. In the sixteenth century, sheets came most frequently in two sizes—the larger measuring about 15″ x 20″, the smaller about 12″ x 16″. If these sheets are printed without any folding, you get what are known as "broadsheets" or "broadsides." Obviously, a book of this size would be very unwieldy and, consequently, "broadsheet" printing is usually confined to proclamations or brief announcements of spectacular events. Since these would normally be pasted on the walls for people to read, they are usually only printed on one side. The front of the sheet is known as the "recto"; the reverse is known as the "verso." A literary—or semi-literary—use of the "broadside" was to print ballads, which would then be hawked around the streets by itinerant singers.

If the original sheet is folded in half vertically, you get the "Folio" format, comprising *two* "leaves" or *four* sides or "pages" per sheet. Thus, on the recto, or outside of the sheet, pages one and four are printed side by side; on the verso, or inside, are printed pages two and three; then the sheet is folded inwards down the middle to give the correct page order—1, 2, 3, 4. All printing on the outside of the sheet is known as the "outer forme"; printing on the inside of the sheet is called the "inner forme." Folio is a favourite size for books of some length, which would be made up of a series of "folio" foldings sewn together along the fold. Each such folded sheet is known as a "gathering"; and the first page of each "gathering" is given an alphabetical letter, according to order, to help the binder to sew the gatherings in the right sequences—gathering "a," gathering "b," gathering "c," etc. These alphabetical signs occur at the foot of the first page of each folio gathering, and are called "signatures." In many early books they are the only indication of page order, since pagination—numbering of each individual page—did not come in till later, and tended not to be accurate even then.

If the sheet, already folded lengthways like a folio, is folded in half again, this time horizontally, top to bottom, you get a "quarto" format, consisting of *four* leaves or *eight* pages per gathering—with pages 1, 4, 5 and 8 on the "outer forme" and pages 2, 3, 6 and 7 on the "inner forme." The alphabetical "signatures" now have to serve several purposes: besides helping to order the sequence of the gatherings in binding, they must ensure correct "imposition"—that is, the correct placing of each page in its "forme" (no easy job, now that the pages of

a "forme" no longer run chronologically)—and also the
correct folding of the completed sheet. Accordingly,
besides the "signatures" at the bottom of the first page
of each gathering, you will find that quarto formats
have additional guiding "signatures" at the foot of each
third and each fifth page. Thus, the first gathering of a
quarto will be signed as follows: page 1—signed "a";
page 2 (verso of page 1)—unsigned; page 3—signed
"a2"; page 4 (verso of page 3)—unsigned; page 5—
signed "a3"; page 6 (verso of page 5)—unsigned. (By the
time that pages 1 to 6 have been "imposed" correctly
or folded in order, the last two pages will automatically
have to fall in the right place; so page 7 is normally unsigned, though you may occasionally find examples of
"a4.") Then the same process is repeated with the
second gathering, this time using the letter "b"—and
so on.

"Versos"—the pages on the reverse of each of the four
leaves in a quarto gathering—are left unsigned. Naturally, if the rectos are correctly folded, the versos will
automatically fall into place; as for "imposition," the
man who makes up the "formes" has a second guide,
besides "signatures," which helps him with versos and
provides a supplementary indication of order for signatured pages. This second guide is the "catchword" convention, by which, after the last line of type at the bottom of each page, the first word of the *next* page is
printed—as an indication, both to reader and printer, of
what is to follow.

If the quarto folding is folded in half again, vertically,
you get the "octavo" format comprising *eight* leaves and
sixteen sides or pages, signatured on pages 1, 3, 5, 7, 9

to ensure correct "imposition" and folding. If you then fold the "octavo" in half horizontally, you get the "decimosexto," of *sixteen* leaves and *thirty-two* pages. If you then fold the "decimosexto" ... you normally get a mess! Any larger folding than "decimosexto" needs a bigger sheet to begin with. Most modern foldings are very elaborate because machines can handle larger sheets than men can.

A more complicated folding is the "duodecimo" folding of *twelve* leaves and *twenty-four* pages, where the original sheet is first folded horizontally into a Z-shape, then twice folded in half vertically. And this is doubled by the 24mo! However, these foldings are difficult to describe without actual demonstration, so, having just mentioned them, I will go on to describe the actual press, a picture of which may be seen on the title page illustration to Geoffrey of Monmouth's *Britanniae Utriusque* (1517), in the Fisher collection. (Plate 2.)

IV

Again, time forces me to simplify somewhat: enthusiasts should consult Chapter 5 of R. B. McKerrow's *An Introduction to Bibliography*. Basically, the Elizabethan press looks rather like a guillotine. That is, two vertical posts (called the "cheeks") are bolted into floor and ceiling. A horizontal table about 2½ feet high runs between them, jutting out at either end. On runners on this table lies the bed of the press, a smooth stone in a wooden frame (called the "coffin"), which can be worked on in the open and then slid in under the actual press. The latter is a smooth piece of metal (the "platen") at the end of a very large vertical screw which runs through a horizontal bar placed between the two up-rights (cheeks). The threads of this screw are very wide, and the "platen" is kept only half an inch above the bed of the press, so that it only needs one half-turn of the vertical screw to bring the "platen" firmly down into the bed of the press. This half-turn is accomplished by means of a bar set horizontally into the screw itself, which the printer just pulls sideways when he wants the screw to turn and the "platen" to be lowered. The resili-ence of the wood causes the screw to spring back to its former position once the bar is released; so that the "coffin" can be slid easily out into the open again after each pressing.

The sequence of Elizabethan printing, therefore, is as follows. First a compositor sets the author's text up, composing line by line on a slotted stick held in his left hand (and working mirror-like, from right to left, so that the line will come out correctly when printed.) He com-poses until enough lines to fill a page have been com-posed, then begins another page. When all the pages constituting a "forme" (one side of a whole sheet) are ready, they are locked together by a frame called the "chace," and placed on the stone bed of the press, where they are inked by means of two ink balls—like cloth mushrooms—which are rubbed in ink and then dabbed over the type. Hinged to the side of the "coffin" (the frame which holds the stone on which the "chace" of type is now resting) is a wooden frame called the "tympanum" which can be bent over to cover the top of the type like a lid. Accordingly, on the inside of this "tympanum" is fastened the sheet of paper to be printed; a light, hollow frame (the "friskit"!) is fastened over this to keep the margins clear; then the "tympanum" is swung down onto the type, like a lid, so that the paper rests on the inked type. (When I was a student, one of two eccentric scholars who were competing to demonstrate a model of the press to us, incautiously put his hand down on the type at this point . . .) The whole "coffin" is then slid along the table under the "platen." The printer pulls the handle which turns the screw and brings the "platen" down firmly on the "tympanum," printing the sheet of paper! (. . . At this point, the rival professor gleefully printed "Season's Greetings" on the first professor's palm!) The handle flies back; the "coffin" is slid out; the printed sheet is removed and hung up to dry; and the whole process is repeated until enough copies have been printed off. The type is then changed—the compositor having been composing all this while—and the dry sheets, now printed on one side or "forme," are "perfected"—that is, the other, blank side or "forme" is printed too. The process then begins all over again on a new gathering.

Now, during this time, the text is several times checked for errors. Before the first copy is printed, the printer quickly reads the type off backwards in the "chace," a trick still practised by modern printers, on the lookout for such obvious errors as inverted letters, misplaced capitals, and wrong type. Then, after the first half dozen or so "pulls," there is a second check: the proofreader will pick up one of the wet sheets and quickly read it over, looking for errors. If such are found, the press is stopped and the type corrected before continuing. This may happen several times during the printing of a single "forme," particularly if the edition is a large one or if the author decides to see his book through the press personally (though this latter was quite rare). Each time errors are found, the press is stopped and the type corrected. *But*—and here comes the difficulty—the Elizabethan printer *does not discard the early, incorrect sheets!* He piles them up with the later, corrected ones, and uses them *all* in the edition! Since each "forme" of a sheet may have been corrected several times during printing, and since the sheets are bound up together quite indiscriminately—corrected sheets of gathering "a" with faulty sheets of gathering "b," etc.—it will be seen that almost limitless permutations of corrected and uncorrected readings are possible for any existing Elizabethan book!

The position is further complicated by the possibility of stop-press corrections made either because the author has changed his mind or—more probably—because it is found that he is offending the government censorship laws or laying himself open to a libel suit. Some copies of the edition may have the original deleted passage; others may have a new, inoffensive version. Sometimes the correction will be inserted after the whole book is printed but before binding—new pages being inserted, which are called a "cancel." Obviously, these can be very important for critical interpretation; but they are only to be located after careful bibliographical examination of the differences of paper!

Play texts tend to exhibit more errors than other kinds of book, simply because the copy text from which the printer worked was more illegible than usual. Theatre companies did not, as a rule, bother much about printing their plays; and when they did, they rarely let the best manuscripts out of their possession. In some cases, the printer has obviously had to do his best with the author's "foul papers"—that is, his original scrawled notes and first draft! Even when the printer has a clear text to work from—a fair copy, say, or even an earlier printed edition—this is often made difficult to follow because it has been used as a prompt book, and is scrawled over with non-authorial production notes and cuts. Moreover, if the fair copy was made by a professional scrivener, *he* may have misread the original anyhow. Some of the copy from which plays were printed was even "pirated"! Actors, isolated in the provinces or hard up in London, would get together and try to *reconstruct* a play from memory—with all the inevitable omissions, transpositions, weakenings and vulgarization to which such a method is prone. Examples of "pirated" texts of Shakespeare are *The Contention between the Houses of York and Lancaster* and *The True Tragedy of Richard, Duke of York*, which are memorial reconstructions of *Parts 2 and 3, Henry VI*, respectively. *Love's Labour's Lost* also appeared originally in such a pirated text, though no copy of this is now extant.

Even if we do not consider the further problem of changes introduced into later editions—were they by the author or someone else?—even disregarding this, enough has been said, I think, to show the complexity which faces any editor of an Elizabethan text, and especially of a play text, the almost endless possible permutations of correct and incorrect readings, and thus the unique value of *every* copy of an Elizabethan book.

V

How then does the modern bibliographer attack this problem, instead of just giving up in despair like earlier editors and printing whatever readings suit him personally?

In the first place, he has to "collate" (read and compare) all the early editions and decide which is the most reliable. Generally, later editions tend to be mechanical reprints of earlier editions, merely multiplying errors; but, in some cases, later editions are more reliable than earlier ones. The bibliographer, therefore, not only has to decide the order in which editions appeared, but has to try to discover what kind of copy each edition derives from—that is, just how far removed the printer's copy was from the author's own manuscript. When he has decided which existing edition is closest to the author's manuscript, the bibliographer then concentrates on that one: it becomes his copytext.

He then has to collate every extant copy of that edition, line by line, comma by comma; not only to record every variant reading in the whole edition, but also to be able to decide exactly how the edition was printed—how many times the press was stopped for each "forme" to be corrected, and even by *whom* the corrections were probably made—compositor, proofreader, or author. This collation of minute details is so tiring and time-consuming that Professor Hinman, who is working on *all* the variants in the Shakespeare Folio of 1623, has invented a special machine to make the task easier. Otherwise it would take him fifty years.

The bibliographer-editor then has to decide which of the many variants are probably most correct; and this involves an exhaustive analysis of how the other, incorrect variants may have arisen. Ideally, no reading should be rejected until the precise means by which it became an error is known. The first step in this analysis is to see whether certain errors might not have arisen through misreading of the copytext manuscript; and since Elizabethan "secretary" handwriting was very different from modern[2], this step is, in itself, a very intricate art—the art of paleography. Professor Sisson who lectured here last year is an expert in this field. It helps, of course, if one knows who wrote the manuscript. Several of Shakespeare's plays reached the printer via the professional scrivener, Ralph Crane, and, thanks to Sir Walter Greg, enough is now known of Crane's writing and reading habits to discount certain peculiarities of texts derived from his handwriting.

A second step is to use one's knowledge of Elizabethan printing to eliminate certain recognizable printing-house errors. Compositors, for example, are prone to "eyeskip": that is, when two sequent lines both end with the same word, the compositor tends to omit the second line. (This is an error you may be familiar with from typing.) Certain compositors, moreover, have a tendency to certain kinds of error; and, by a statistical analysis of *all* texts printed in a certain printing house during a certain space of time, these errors can frequently be isolated, and thus discounted. (Though, statistics being

---

[2] For examples of Elizabethan handwriting, see the illustrations to Sergeant Huber's article on "The Booke of Sir Thomas More" in *Stratford Papers on Shakespeare*, I (1960).

what they are, this approach can lead to weird results, like Professor Dover Wilson's assertion that a "left-handed Welshman" had a hand—presumably the left one—in *Hamlet*.) Then there are certain purely mechanical errors that can be identified and also discounted: the type can get mixed up, for instance, in the racks from which the compositor takes it to compose; or, in inking the type with the clumsy ink balls, letters may be loosened or even pulled clean out.

Lastly, there is the problem of over-correction. Much of the press correction was done by non-literary artisans working purely by eye without reference to the original copytext. One result, inevitably, is simplification. The corrector, in other words, meets a difficult passage which needs much pondering before the sense is clear, and, not having time to ponder, he assumes that there is a mistake and changes it to something more easily comprehensible—which, nevertheless, falsifies the author's intention. A particular compositor's tendency to do this can be worked out statistically if enough texts set by him exist to be analyzed.

When we reach this last realm of editing, however, the objective, "scientific" approach which I have been stressing once more merges into the subjective, "eclectic" method of the early editors. It just isn't possible to arrive at 100% objective accuracy in editing an Elizabethan text. There never will be a perfect edition of Shakespeare, and sooner or later the value of any particular edition will depend on the editor's individual taste and insight. Editing is still an art, not a science. But this area of doubt, this no-man's land (or rather, this every man's land!), is far less extensive than it used

Plate 1: Portrait of Shakespeare from the title page of the First Folio of 1623. The dimensions of the portrait are 6.3″ by 7.5″. The copperplate engraving is by Martin Droeshout, a Flemish engraver living in London, who was then about 22. The drawing from which he worked is unknown. With all its imperfections, the engraving agrees well with the only other portrait possessing any authenticity, the Stratford bust. The greatest treasure of English literature, the First Folio was published in an edition of about 600 copies, of which nearly 200 survive. Shakespeare died in 1616.

Plate 2: Title page of *Britanniae Utriusque* by Geoffrey of Monmouth, Paris, 1517. This was printed by the great French printer Badius Ascensius, and the woodcut shows his shop. This is one of the earliest illustrations of printers at work: at the left is the pressman, at the centre the inker and at the right the compositor. Shakespeare's stories of *Cymbeline* and *King Lear* were derived from Geoffrey, through Holinshed. Dimensions of illustration 2.5″ by 3.2″.

(a)

(b)

Frigida pugnabant calidis, humentia siccis,
Mollia cum duris, sine pondere habentia pondus.
Hanc deus et melior litem natura diremit.
Nam ... ego terras, et terris abscidit undas
Et liquidum spisso secreuit ab aethere caelum.
Quae postquam euoluit, caecisq; exemit aceruo,
Dissociata locis concordi pace ligauit.

(c)

ER qual mio destino dirò io,
Senatori, auenire, che niuno
per questi uint'anni sia stato
nemico della Republica, ilqua-
le nel medesimo tempo non
habbia ancora sopra di me
bandita la guerra? ne è di ne-
cessità, che io nomini alcuno, ricordateueli uoi
medesimi. essi m'hanno dato piu che fare, che
io non desideraua. di te Antonio mi marauiglio,

(d)

6 So the woman (seeing that the tree was good for meate, and that it was pleasant to the eies, and a tree to be desired to get knowledge) tooke of the fruite thereof, and did eate, and gaue also to her husband with her, and he did eate.
7 Then the eyes of them both were opened, and they knewe that they were naked, and they sewed figge tree leaues together, and made themselues breeches.
8 ¶ Afterward they heard the voyce of the Lorde God walking in the garden in the coole of the day, and the man and his wife ...

22 ¶ And the Lord God said, Beholde, man is become as one of vs, to knowe good and euill. And nowe lest he put foorth his hande, and take also of the tree of life, and eate and liue for euer,
23 Therefore the Lord God sent him foorth from the garden of Eden, to till the earth whence he was taken.
24 Thus hee cast out man, and at the East side of the garden of Eden set the cherubims, and the blade of a sworde shaken, to keepe the way of the tree of life.

(e)

14 The labour of the foolish is grieuous vnto them, while they knowe not how to goe into the citie.
15 Woe be vnto thee, O thou land, whose King is but a childe, and whose princes are earely at their banquets.
16 But well is thee, O thou land, whose King is come of nobles, and whose princes eate in due season for necessitie, and not for lust.

Plate 3: Early type faces.

(a) The first edition of Plutarch's *Lives*, printed at Venice in 1519 by Aldus. This was the first Greek type face cut. Shakespeare drew the plots of his Roman plays from Plutarch in North's English translation, 1579.

(b) Ovid's *Metamorphoses*, printed by Aldus at Venice in 1502, is one of the earliest examples of italic type, devised by Aldus a few months earlier.

(c) Aldus' first roman type, from his Italian *Philippics of Cicero* printed at Venice in 1556.

(d) The Geneva Bible, printed at London in 1594. In England secular books had largely changed over to roman type but religious books still retained Gothic. This was the Breeches Bible, so called from the last word of the passage at Genesis III 7 shown. In other editions the word is "aprons."

(e) The Bishops' Bible, printed at London in 1585. In *Richard III* a citizen says, "Woe to that land that's governed by a child," which is taken from the passage at Ecclesiastes X 15 shown.

(a)

(b)

Plate 4: Early handwriting.

(a) This is a page of 15th-century monkish writing, and is the model on which the early printers cut their types.

(b) Italian handwriting, which we use today was introduced into England during Shakespeare's lifetime, but Shakespeare and most of his contemporaries continued to write an "English" hand. This plate is from the 1620 manuscript of Sir George Buck's *History of Richard the Third*, and shows a handsome example of the writing of the day. The excerpt reads as follows:

" . . . for the ignorant and never understanding vulgare, whose faith (in history) is drawn from Pamphlet, and Ballad; and theire Reverend and learned Authors, the stage or those that play the bauds to it, for a liveinge, let them flye theire owne pitch; for they are but kytes, and dawes, and can digest naught (soe well) as stench and filth; to wch I leave them . . . "

This passage most probably refers to Shakespeare and his company. Buck was the official who licensed a number of Shakespeare's plays, including *Richard III*, for performance.

Plate 5: This is one of 46 illustrations in Sir John Harington's English translation of 1591 of Ariosto's *Orlando Furioso*. These were the first copper engravings made in England. Shakespeare knew *Orlando* well, and it is probable that this illustration showing the rocky island, the hermit, his sprite, the monsters, the shipwrecked gallants and the maiden provided some of the stuff from which *The Tempest* was fashioned.

(a)

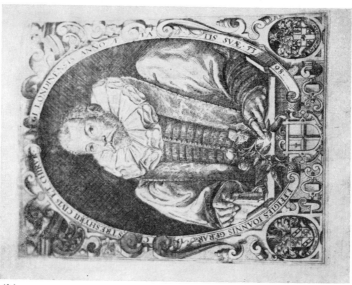

(b)

Plate 6: Elizabethan worthies. These two portraits have been chosen because they show the handsome and intelligent faces of two men of eminence, who are almost unknown to the general reader today. John Florio (1553-1625), was the author of Italian-English dictionaries and the first English translator of Montaigne's *Essays.* Shapespeare knew these books well, and must have known their author. The portrait of Florio is from his 1613 edition of Montaigne. John Gerard (1545-1612), published in 1597 a monumental work on plants, to which Shakespeare made many references throughout the plays. This portrait, from the book, shows Gerard holding the then newly-discovered potato plant. Gerard was examiner for the Barber-Surgeons Company, whose headquarters were directly across the street from the house where Shakespeare lived for some years.

Plate 7: Saxton's Map of Warwickshire. This is the first printed map of Warwickshire, the county in which Shakespeare was born and died. It shows Warwickshire in 1576; Shakespeare was then 12. This map was republished many times during a period of nearly 200 years. Dimensions 14.0″ by 12.0″.

(a)

(b)

Plate 8: Early wood-cut illustrations.

(a) Shakespeare's principal source for the ten English historical plays was Raphael Holinshed's *Chronicles* of 1577, which consists of two thick folio volumes, enriched with thousands of wood-cuts. This plate shows an illustration Shakespeare must have pored over, of Macbeth and Banquo meeting the three witches. Holinshed's text adjoining the illustration, including the "All hail, Macbeth" speeches of the witches, was taken over almost verbatim by Shakespeare. Dimensions 5.2″ by 3.1″.

(b) Chaucer's *Knight's Tale*. This is from the 1561 edition of Chaucer's works, the edition which Shakespeare apparently knew. This plate is an excellent example of English printing in the middle of the 16th century. From *The Knight's Tale* Shakespeare derived the Theseus theme in *A Midsummer Night's Dream*, and the plot of *The Two Noble Kinsmen*.

to be, thanks to the growth of modern bibliography. And bibliography could not function without access to original texts such as these of Mr. Fisher's collection. It is thanks to these inaccurate "old books" that we now have more accurate texts of Shakespeare than even the Elizabethans had.

AN EXHIBIT OF SHAKESPEARE BOOKS FROM SIDNEY FISHER'S COLLECTION.

Exhibited at the Stratford (Ontario) Shakespearean Festival, 1961.

EDITIONS OF SHAKESPEARE'S WORKS

Mr. William Shakespeare's Comedies, Histories, and Tragedies. London, 1623. First Folio.

Mr. William Shakespeare's Comedies, Histories, and Tragedies. London, 1632. Second Folio.

Mr. William Shakespeare's Comedies, Histories, and Tragedies. London, 1664. Third Folio.

Mr. William Shakespeare's Comedies, Histories, and Tragedies. London, 1685. Fourth Folio.

Shakespeare's Plays, Nicolas Rowe, Editor. London, 1709. Seven volumes. Fifth edition.

William Shakespeare, A Collection of Poems. London, 1709. Two issues. Second edition.

William Shakespeare, A Collection of Poems. London, 1709-10. Third edition.

William Shakespeare, Poems, London, 1710. Fourth edition.

Shakespeare's Works, Lewis Theobald, Editor. London, 1733. Eight volumes.

SOURCE BOOKS

Ovid, *Metamorphoses*. Venice, 1502. Lyons, 1529. Antwerp, 1582. Three editions.

Ovid, *Fasti, De Tristibus* and *De Ponto*. Venice, 1503; Venice, 1533; Antwerp, 1582. Three editions.

Geoffrey of Monmouth, *Britanniae Utriusque*. Paris, 1517. London, 1718.

Titus Livius, *History of Rome*. Venice, 1519.

Plutarch, *Lives* (in Greek). Venice, 1519.

Lucius Apuleius, *De Asino Aureo*. Venice, 1521.

Boethius, *Scotorum Historia*. Paris, 1527.

Ovid, *Heroides*. Lyons, 1528. Antwerp, 1578. Two editions.

Homer, *Odyssey* (Greek). Strasburg, 1534.

Plinius Secundus, *Naturalis Historiae*. Venice, 1535, three volumes, (Aldus). Lyons, 1560, four volumes, (Junta).

Homer, *Iliad* (Latin). Venice, 1537.

Giovanni Boccaccio, *Il Decamerone*. Venice, 1542.

Baldassare Castiglione, *Il Cortegiano*. Lyons, 1562. Venice, 1545. Two editions.

Cicero, *Philippics* against Mark Antony (Italian). Venice, 1546.

William Langland, *The Vision of Pierce Ploughman*. London, 1550.

Edward Halle, *Union of Lancastre and Yorke*. London, 1550. Two copies.

John Lydgate, *The Fall of Princes*. London, 1554.

Plautus, *Comoediae Viginti*. Leyden, 1554.

Sir Thomas Elyot, *The Boke Named the governour*. London, 1557.

Ser Giovanni, *Il Pecorone*. Milan, 1558.

Robert Fabian, *Chronicle*. London, 1559.

Geoffrey Chaucer, *Woorkes*. London, 1561.

Ludovico Ariosto, *Comedie*. Venice, 1562.

Giovanni Battista Giraldi Cinthio, *Gli Hecatommithi*. Ferrara, 1565. Two volumes.

Sir Thomas North, *The Diall of Princes*. London, 1568.

Richard Grafton, *A Chronicle . . . of Englande.* 1568-9.

Sire Jehan Froissart, *Histoire et Chronique.* Paris, 1574. Two copies.

Raphael Holinshed, *The Chronicles of England, Scotlande and Irelande.* London, 1577. Two volumes.

François de Belle Forest, *Histoires Tragiques.* Lyons, 1578.

Plutarch, *Les vies des Hommes Illustres Grecs et Romains,* Trad. par M. Jacques Amyot. Paris, 1579. Two copies.

Sir Thomas North, *The Lives of the Noble Grecians and Romanes by Plutarke.* London, 1579.

Giovanni Battista Giraldi Cinthio, *Epitia Tragedia.* Venice, 1583.

The Holy Byble. (The Bishop's Bible). London, 1585.

Virgil, *Eclogues, Georgics* and *Aeneid.* Venice, 1586.

Sir John Ferne, *The Blazon of Gentrie.* London, 1586.

William Camden, *Britannia.* London, 1590, 1594 and 1600. Three editions.

Sir John Harington, *Orlando Furioso.* London, 1591.

The Bible (The Geneva Bible). London, 1594.

Giovanni Boccaccio, *Le Decameron,* translated in French by Antoine le Macon. Lyons, 1597.

John Gerarde, *The Herball or Generall Historie of Plantes.* London, 1597. Two copies. London, 1636. Two editions.

John Florio, *A Worlde of Wordes.* London, 1598.

John Manwood, *The Lawes of the Forrest.* London, 1598. Two copies.

Livy, *The Romaine Historie.* Translated by Philemon Holland. London, 1600.

Pliny, *The Historie of the World.* Translated by Philemon Holland. London, 1601.

Lodovico Ariosto, *Orlando Furioso.* Venice, 1603.

William Camden, *Remaines.* London, 1607.

Edmund Spenser, *The Faerie Queene.* London, 1609.

George Turberville, *The Noble Art of Venerie.* London, 1611.

Montaigne, *Essayes,* translated into English by John Florio. London, 1613. Two copies.

Sir Philip Sidney, *Works*. London, 1627.
John Lyly, *Euphues. Euphues and his England*.
London, 1631.
John Peter Camus, *Admirable Events,* translated by
S. du Verger. London, 1639.
Saxo Grammaticus, *Historia Danica*. Sora, 1644.
Sir John Skeffington, *The Heroe, of Lorenzo*. London, 1652.
The Book of Common Prayer. Oxford, 1719.
Thomas Middleton, *The Witch*. London, 1778.
William Lily, *Latin Grammar*. London, no date.

ALLUSION BOOKS

William Camden, *Remaines Concerning Britaine*. London,
seven editions dated from 1607 to 1674.
Benjamin Jonson, *Workes*. London, 1616. Two copies.
Edmund Spenser, *Colin Clouts Come Home Againe*.
London, 1617.
Sir George Buck, *The History of Richard The Third*.
Manuscript. 1620.
John Weever, *Ancient Funerall Monuments*. London, 1631.
Two copies.
John Stow, *Annales*. London, 1631.
John Speed, *Historie of Great Britaine*. London, 1632.
John Fox, *Acts and Monuments of the Christian Martyrs*.
London, 1634. Three volumes.
Thomas Heywood, *Hierarchie of the Blessed Angels*.
London, 1635.
John Swan, *Speculum Mundi*. Cambridge, 1635.
Thomas Robinson, *The Anatomie of the English Nunnery
at Lisbon*. London, 1637.
Benjamin Jonson, *Workes*. London, 1640. Four copies.
Sir Richard Baker, *A Chronicle of the Kings of England*.
London, 1643. Three copies.
Sir George Buck, *The History of Richard III*. London, 1646.
Sir John Suckling, *Fragmenta Aurea*. London, 1648. Three
copies.

King Charles II, *Eikon Basilike*. London, 1648.

John Milton, *Eikonoclastes*. London, 1649.

Thomas Fuller, *The Church History of Britain*.
London, 1655.

William Dugdale, *The Antiquities of Warwickshire*.
London, 1656.

Thomas Fuller, *The History of the Worthies of England*.
London, 1662.

David Lloyd, *Statesmen and Favourites of England*.
London, 1670.

Sir William Davenant, *Works*. London, 1673.

John Milton, *Poems*. London, 1673.

Edward Phillips, *Theatrum Poetarum*. London, 1675.

Scarron's *Comical Romance*. London, 1676. Two copies.

Robert Burton, *The Anatomy of Melancholy*. London, 1676.
Two copies.

Abraham Cowley, *Works*. London, 1680.

William Winstanley, *England's Worthies*. London, 1684.

John Dryden, *Works*. London, 1687-95. Four volumes.

Gerard Langbaine, *An Account of the English Dramatic
Poets*. Oxford, 1691.

Sir Thomas Blount, *De Re Poetica*. London, 1694.

William Wycherley, *The Country Wife*. London, 1695.

John Milton, *Works*. London, 1697. | Two copies.

Jeremy Collier, *Short View of the English Stage*, etc.
London, 1698.

Jeremy Collier, *Defence of the Short View, etc.*
London, 1699.

William Drummond, *Works*. Edinburgh, 1711. Two copies.

Sir William Dugdale, *Antiquities of Warwickshire*.
London, 1730.

Colley Cibber, *An Apology for the Life of Colley Cibber*.
London, 1740.

W. R. Chetwood, *A General History of the Stage*.
London, 1749.

Richard Farmer, *The Learning of Shakespeare.*
    London, 1767.
Thomas Arne, *An Ode to Shakespeare.* London, 1769.
John Aubrey, *Lives of Eminent Men.* London, 1813.
    Three volumes.

ILLUSTRATIONS

Early Fifteenth Century Manuscript. (Leaf)
Hartmann Schedel, *Liber Chronicarum.* Nuremberg, 1493.
    (Leaf)
Sebastian Brant, *Stultifera Navis.* Strasburg, 1497. (Leaf)
Francesco Petrarca, *Sonetti e Canzoni.* Venice, 1538.
The Workes of Geoffrey Chaucer. London, 1542.
    (Double leaf)
The Workes of Geoffrey Chaucer. London, 1550.
    (Double leaf)
Sebastian Muenster, Map of England, 1552.
Thomas Cooper, *Thesaurus,* etc. London, 1565.
William Lambarde, *A Perambulation of Kent.* London, 1576.
Blaise de Vigenère,*Traicté des Chiffres.* Paris, 1586.
Rerum Britannicarum. Heidelberg, 1587.
Brooke, *A Discoverie . . . of Certaine Errours.* London, 1596.
John Hayward, *The Life and raigne of King Henrie the IIII.*
    London, 1599.
William Camden, *Anglica, Normannica,* etc. Frankfurt, 1603.
John Stow, *Summarie of the English Chronicle.*
    London, 1607.
Robert Glover, *Nobilitas Politica vel Civilis.* London, 1608.
    Two copies.
Thomas Milles, *The Catalogue of Honor.* London, 1610.
    Three copies.
Thomas Coryat, *Coryat's Crudities.* London, 1611.
William Hole, Map of Warwickshire. 1612.
Richard Bernard, *Terence in English.* London, 1614.
Sir Walter Ralegh, *The Historie of the World.* London, 1614.
William Camden, *Annales Regnante Elizabetha.*
    London, 1615.

Fynes Moryson, *An Itinerary.* London, 1617.

John Stow, *The Survay of London.* London, 1618.

Ralph Brooke, *A Catalogue ... of the Kings.* London, 1619.

Augustine Vincent, *Errours of—Brooke.* London, 1622.

André Favine, *The Theater of Honour and Knighthood.*
London, 1623.

William Camden, *Annales,* etc. Leyden. 1625. (Latin)

Samuel Purchas, *Pilgrimes.* London, 1625. Four volumes.

Samuel Purchas, *Pilgrimage.* London, 1626.

George Chapman, *Caesar and Pompey.* London, 1631.

Henry Cockeram, *The English Dictionarie.* London, 1631.

Thomas Fuller, *History of the Holy Warre.* Cambridge,
1640. Two copies.

Thomas Fuller, *The Holy State.* Cambridge, 1642. Two
copies.

John Speed, Map of England. Amsterdam, 1643.

Jan Jansson, Map of Warwickshire, 1646.

Francis Beaumont and John Fletcher, *Works.* London, 1647.

Edward Herbert, Lord Cherbury, *King Henry the Eighth.*
London, 1649 and 1683.

Isaac Walton, *Life of Sir Henry Wotton.* London, 1651.

Sir Henry Wotton, *Reliquiae Wottonianae.* London, 1651.

Sir William Dugdale, *History of St. Paul's Cathedral.*
London, 1658 and 1716. Two editions.

Sir Henry Wotton, *Reliquiae Wottonianae.* London, 1685.
Two copies.

James Howell, *Familiar Letters.* London, 1678.

John Guilim, *A Display of Heraldrie.* London, 1679.

Francis Beaumont and John Fletcher, *Works.* London, 1679.

Nicholas Ling, *Wits Commonwealth.* London, 1688.

William Camden, *History of Princess Elizabeth.*
London, 1688.

William Camden, *Annales,* etc. London, 1688. (English)

Sir Roger L'Estrange, *Fables of Aesop.* London, 1692.

John Dryden, *Poems.* London, 1700 and 1701.

Ralph Brooke, *A Discoverie of Errours,*
William Camden, *Answer to Ralph Brooke,*

Ralph Brooke, *A Second Discoverie of Errours.*
London, 1723.
Count Castiglione, *The Courtier.* London, 1724.
Lewis Theobald, *Shakespeare Restored.* London, 1726.
Lewis Theobald, *Double Falsehood.* London, 1728.
John Hales, *A Brief Examination,* etc. London, 1751.
Samuel Johnson, *A Dictionary of the English Language.*
London, 1755. Two volumes.
Thomas Percy, *Reliques of Ancient English Poetry.* London,
1765. Three volumes.
Elizabeth Montagu, *Writings and Genius of Shakespeare.*
London, 1769.
Thomas Kyd, *Arden of Feversham.* London, 1770.
Maurice Morgann, *Sir John Falstaff.* London, 1777.
Isaac Walton, *Lives.* London, 1796.
Edmund Malone, *An Account of —Shakespeare's Tempest.*
London, 1808.
William Hazlitt, *English Comic Writers.* London, 1819.
Theatra Illustrata. London, 1825.
Franz Schubert, *Staendchen.* Vienna, 1830.

HOAXES, etc.

W. H. Ireland, *Miscellaneous Papers . . . of William
Shakespeare.* London, 1796.
James Boaden, *A Letter to George Steevens,* London, 1796.
George Chalmers, *An Apology for the Believers in the
Shakespeare Papers.* London, 1797.
George Chalmers, *A Supplemental Apology.* London, 1799.
W. H. Ireland, *Confessions.* London, 1805.
Richard Fenton, *A Tour in Quest of Genealogy.* London,
1811. Two copies.
J. Payne Collier, *Notes and Emendations,* etc. London, 1852.
N. E. S. A. Hamilton, *An Inquiry into the Manuscript
Corrections,* etc. London, 1860.
Oscar Wilde, *The Portrait of Mr. W. H.* Edinburg, 1889.
E. D. Johnson, *Mystery of the First Folio.* Birmingham,
no date.

The distinguished American Renaissance scholar, Alfred Bennett Harbage, was the principal lecturer in the second seminar. A graduate, both actual and honorary, of the University of Pennsylvania, he has held the rank of Professor of English there and at Columbia University and, since 1952, at Harvard. He is, too, a Fellow of the American Academy of Arts and Science. His published works include many specifically concerned with Shakespeare and the theatre: *Annals of English Drama, Shakespeare's Audience, As They Liked It, Shakespeare and the Rival Traditions,* and *Theatre for Shakespeare* (the 1955 Alexander Lectures in the University of Toronto). He is general editor of the Pelican Shakespeare and has prepared editions of several of the plays for that series.

ALFRED HARBAGE

Love's Labor's Lost

AND THE EARLY SHAKESPEARE *

After remarking that Sir Edmund Chambers, "the
very pink of orthodoxy and paragon of caution," declines to recognize any date earlier than 1590-91 for
Shakespeare's extant work, F. P. Wilson continues,

> The fact is that the chronology of Shakespeare's
> earliest plays is so uncertain that it has no right to
> harden into an orthodoxy, and perhaps we should do
> better to say that by 1592 he had certainly written
> *Henry VI* (all three parts), *Richard III*, *The Comedy
> of Errors*, probably *Titus Andronicus* and possibly *The
> Taming of the Shrew*, and that the earliest of these
> may have been written as early as 1588.[1]

The statement, like the delightful book in which it appears, is liberal in intention, but it is tinged with the
orthodoxy which it gently rebukes. As it proceeds from
"certainly" to "probably" to "possibly," still excluding
Love's Labor's Lost, it seems to sound an irrevocable
doom. At the beginning of the eighteenth century *Love's
Labor's Lost* was considered Shakespeare's first (and

*The lecture here appears in slightly altered form, as revised and documented
for publication; reprinted by courtesy of the editors, P.Q. XLI, no. 1, 1962
(*Studies in English Drama Presented to Baldwin Maxwell*).

worst) play. At the end of the nineteenth, although "worst" was no longer a permissible word in Shakespearean commentary, the best Shakespeare scholars were convinced that "the first draft of the comedy must have been written when the author was a youth."[2] These "best scholars" were F. J. Furnivall, presiding genius of the New Shakspere Society; F. G. Fleay, indefatigable analyst of versification and sundry clues; A. W. Ward, leading historian of the English drama; and Sir Sidney Lee, Shakespeare's "definitive" biographer. Their date for the play was 1587-90. "To *Love's Labor's Lost*," said Lee decisively, "may reasonably be assigned priority in point of time of all Shakespeare's dramatic productions."[3] This was the *old* orthodoxy. With equal decisiveness the best scholars of the present century have dated the play in the mid-nineties as one of the lyrical group. This is the *new* orthodoxy.

Orthodoxies are begotten of orthodoxies; firm stands on debatable issues are often assumed, at least in part, in reaction to preceding stands. Old opinions are recognizable as articles of belief. New opinions are easily mistaken for fact. Perhaps it is safest to remain moderate in faith.

One of the forces which have led to the re-dating of *Love's Labor's Lost* is the twentieth-century tendency to upgrade plays formerly regarded as unworthy such as *Titus Andronicus* and *Troilus and Cressida*; it is another brand snatched from the burning. In the eighteenth and nineteenth centuries it was considered poor and early. It is no longer considered poor, and hence (small value in this *hence*) no longer considered early. Scholars have insisted, and rightly, that it is poor only if judged by standards inapplicable to it. It is a coterie play, a "courtly" play, and stands naturally in contrast with the popular plays which have established in our minds the Shakespearean norm. So far so good. It is when we ask how a coterie play came to be written during the single interval when there were no coterie theatres (1591-98) that we detect a thinning of the ice. "Doubtless," says Kittredge, "the play was written for performance at court or at some great house."[4] The view is shared by Chambers ("suggests a courtly rather than a popular audience")[5] and by the two most ambitious of its modern editors, Dover Wilson ("written for a private performance in the house of some grandee")[6] and Richard David ("written for private performance in court circles").[7] This is a meagre sampling of current affirmations—which are usually supplemented with suggestions of particular occasions in particular great houses where the play might have seen its birth.

Love's Labor's Lost thus joins the swelling list of plays for which private auspices of production are hypothesized: *Midsummer Night's Dream* for a noble wedding (with various weddings deemed appropriate), *Merry Wives* for an installation fête of the Order of the Garter (with several installations available), *Troilus and Cressida* for a feast at the inns of court (there were four inns and many feasts), and so on. The trouble is that there is nothing to support any of these hypotheses except the other hypotheses, now functioning as ghostly precedents. There is no supporting external evidence to prove that any regular play performed by any regular company, juvenile or adult, was originally written for a special occasion during the whole reign of Elizabeth and lifetime of Shakespeare. This total absence of evidence would be rather remarkable if such plays were as common in fact as they have become in theory. They are the kind of thing (as witness the entertainments offered during Elizabeth's progresses, and the masques at James's court) such as would have left records—in household accounts, in contemporary gossip, and on title pages. Instead we have records like the following:

> I have sent and bene all thys morning huntyng for players, Juglers & Such kinde of Creaturs, but fynde them harde to finde, wherfore Leavinge notes for them to seeke me, Burbage ys come, & Sayes ther ys no new playe that the quene hath not seene, but they have Revyved on olde one, Cawled *Loves Labore lost,* which for wytt & mirthe he sayes will please her excedingly. And Thys ys apointed to be playd to Morowc night at my Lord of Sowthamptons, unless yow send a wrytt to Remove the Corpus Cum Causa to your howse in Strande. Burbage ys my messenger Ready attendyng your pleasure.[8]

The tone of this epistle conveys much truth about the theatrical world of the Elizabethans, who did not accord their great drama quite the respect that we do. That they were willing to accept for their private occasions plays from the regular repertories is proven by *many* records, of the royal court, the inns of court, and the "great houses." The Essex faction, even when in need of a propaganda piece in 1601, settled for *Richard II*, a back-number in the Chamberlain's Men's repertory. In 1599 Henslowe paid Dekker £2 "for the eande of Fortewnates for the corte."[9] He had already paid Dekker £7 for working over the play, which had been in some form or other part of the Admiral's

Men's repertory since at least 1596. A company was willing to invest £2 in presumed royal gratitude, charging the sum against the modest fee they would receive for the court performance, but to buy and mount an entire play would have been another matter. And there is little to suggest that the court, the inns of court, or the great houses would have been willing to underwrite an entire production by professional actors, whose regular wares were available at fixed rates. Moreover, the writing and rehearsing of a play was a considerable undertaking, then as now, requiring more time than was normally available during preparations for a party. It does not follow that there was never a play *ad hoc,* but in view of the difficulties and the absence of records, it is clear that they could not have been common—not common enough surely to supply an easy explanation for the puzzling characteristics of every puzzling play. The burden of proof rests with those who resort to the explanation.

Love's Labor's Lost was duly performed for Queen Anne in 1605 after Burbage made his suggestion. It had probably been performed before Queen Elizabeth under similar circumstances before its publication in 1598— "As it was presented before her Highnes this last Christmas. Newly corrected and augmented By W. Shakespere." The best scholars of the old orthodoxy naïvely read "newly corrected and augmented" to mean that Shakespeare had refurbished a play for the court performance much as Dekker had refurbished *Old Fortunatus.* Several duplicate passages in the text indicate cancels printed in error, and hence revision. The twentieth century has learned to read bibliographical evidence more subtly. The duplicate passages indicate revision in the course of original composition rather than in working over old matter; and the "newly corrected and augmented" may mean that there had been a "bad quarto" (now lost) just as there had been a bad quarto of *Romeo and Juliet* before the publication of the good quarto of 1599. True the latter reads "newly corrected, augmented, and amended," a slightly different thing, but we may admit the virtue of the suggestion.

Oddly enough, however, the new bibliographical findings do not in the least affect the old assumption that the 1598 quarto of *Love's Labor's Lost* represents an early play reworked, although they have seemed to do so to the finders. The duplicate passages indicate alterations during original composition, but only during composition of those parts of the play where they occur. Those parts *in toto* may be revisions, and as a matter of fact there is evidence (generally conceded) of revision of a different kind—structural revision, such as continues to suggest what the duplicate passages used to suggest. And although there may have been a "bad quarto," there is no reason to assume that it resembled the bad quarto of *Romeo and Juliet*, a debased version of the extant text. Since we are only hypothesizing it anyway, we may as well hypothesize something more on the order of *A Shrew, King Leir,* or the *Troublesome Reign,* or even a *good* version of an earlier form of the present play. Even a bad quarto precisely like that of *Romeo and Juliet* would not cancel the possibility that the text it debased had itself been "newly corrected and augmented." That the 1598 quarto of *Love's Labor's Lost* was printed from the author's draft seems to me to have been proved,[10] but this draft may well have in-corporated whole sheets from an earlier draft. Whereas the new findings do not really affect former assumptions, they seem (quaintly) to have prompted a compromise —to the effect that there *was* an early version but *less early* than formerly assumed. Perhaps it seemed waste-ful to offer new data without offering new conclusions.

Of incalculable effect in the dating controversy has been Warburton's fatal surmise of 1747 that Holofernes in *Love's Labor's Lost* represents John Florio. Commen-tators worried this bone for a century and a half, then suddenly filled the air with dust in digging up rival bones. Warburton spoke with irritating certainty, and he was no intellectual giant; it is fitting that his state-ment should have aroused contempt in our times, but one wishes that the contempt had been directed at his mental processes rather than at their product. He should be blamed for the nature of his laboring rather than for his mouse. To him the fact that part of A resembled part of B meant that A was B. It means nothing of the kind, but neither do similar equations mean that A was really C or D or E or F, and so on endlessly. Actually, the sug-gestion that Holofernes is Florio is no worse, and con-siderably better, than most rival suggestions. None of the characters in *Love's Labor's Lost* resemble in other than a generic fashion (and not very much in that) any of the actual persons with whom they have been identi-fied: King Philip, Bishop Cooper, Northumberland, Southampton, Perez, Lyly, Chapman, Ralegh, Harriot, Harvey, Nashe, etc. Not one of the episodes in the play resembles even generically the actual episodes in the Marprelate and Harvey-Nashe controversy, the

Southampton marriage negotiations, the association of Ralegh with suspect intellectuals, etc. The methods used by the expounders of "topicalities" differ only in degree of recklessness from the methods used by Eva Turner Clark in proving that *Love's Labor's Lost* was written by the Earl of Essex in 1578[11] or Abel Lefranc in proving that the earl was not Oxford but Derby.[12] The method is not that of beginning with a mystery and finding a clue, but of beginning with a clue and finding a mystery. None of the advocates of the rival interpretations have been able to convince one another, and all of them collectively should be unable to convince anyone who has passed an elementary course in logic.

So much in way of truth. Immediately we must recognize that most of the expounders have done sound scholarly work of other kinds, and that their work even in this kind is published under respectable auspices.[13] *Love's Labor's Lost* seems to act upon them as catnip acts upon perfectly sane cats, and possibly the fault lies in the play itself. Although its situations are conventional, there is a curious open-endedness about them which sends the fancies groping, and although all its jokes are explicable as jokes, some of them are so execrably bad as to create *hope* for ulterior meanings. And indeed there are some few phrases associated with the persons and topics adduced. Shakespeare used the idiom of his day. There must be other phrases associated with other topics which happily lie too deeply buried for exploitation. Catch-phrases derived from current events do not mean that the writing where they occur has to do with those events, and if the phrases appear in revised writing, they tell us nothing of original date and source of inspiration. Yet the sheer weight of the discussion of "topicalities," most of which date 1590-95, has created a sentiment or "climate of opinion" in favor of a date of original composition in the mid-nineties, even among those who reject the specific findings of the expounders. Perhaps they are unconsciously influenced by the dubious principle that where there is smoke there must be fire, or perhaps they are simply too charitable to remain impervious to so much earnest endeavor. Still a heap of fallacies has no more authority than any one of the fallacies comprising the heap; otherwise Shakespeare would surely be Bacon. The twentieth-century discussion of the "true meaning" of *Love's Labor's Lost,* heretical though it has seemed to conservative scholars such as Chambers and Kittredge, has nevertheless influenced their new orthodoxy in dating the play circa 1595.

It is time for more positive considerations. Anyone who maintains that the original version of the play was written between 1592 and 1597, and probably about 1595, must supply satisfactory answers to several questions. First of all, why does the play contain 228 lines of verse like the following?

> *Princess.* What plume of feathers is he that indited
>   this letter?
> What vane? What weathercock? Did you ever hear
>   better?
> *Boyet.* I am much deceived but I remember the
>   style.
> *Princess.* Else your memory is bad, going o'er it
>   erewhile.
> *Boyet.* This Armado is a Spaniard that keeps here
>   in court,

A phantasime, a Monarcho, and one that makes
    sport
To the Prince and his bookmates.
Princess.   Thou fellow, a word:
Who gave you this letter?
Costard.   I told you—my Lord. (IV.i.93-100)

Nothing resembling such verse appears in *Richard II*,
Midsummer Night's Dream, or *Romeo and Juliet*, the
plays of the lyrical group. Indeed verse of this kind
appears in quantity in only one other place in Shakespeare,[14] in Act I, scene iii of *The Comedy of Errors*,
and there it has been viewed, at least by some, as a fossil
of some quite early anterior version of the play.[15] It is
hard to believe that, having adapted so perfectly to his
purpose blank verse and the heroic couplet in the plays
of the lyrical group (and in parts of *Love's Labor's Lost*
itself) Shakespeare would have relapsed to doggerel,
and considered it appropriate for the witty exchanges
of royal and noble speakers. Dover Wilson, Chambers,
and Kittredge have all spoken, justly, of the poetic
facility of *Love's Labor's Lost* and the maturity of its
blank verse. This means that they have been looking at
less inconvenient passages than the one sampled above.
Looking at such passages, A. W. Ward spoke of the
"peculiarities, not to say crudities, of its versification,"[16]
and W. J. Courthope of the resemblance to "the lumber-
ing metre of the Moralities."[17]

Tumbling measures had been characteristic of the
school drama of Nicholas Udall (*Ralph Roister Doister*,
circa 1553); they persist in the chapel drama of Richard
Edwardes (*Damon and Pythias*, 1565); and as late as
1581-84 appear in Peele's *Arraignment of Paris* per-

formed by the Children of the Chapel while based in their theatre at Blackfriars. In fact the latter play, mingling as it does quatrains, heroic couplets, blank verse, etc., with old-fashioned doggerel, provides the nearest analogy we have to the commixture of measures in *Love's Labor's Lost*. Lyly's plays for the boy companies in the eighties were written in prose, but one can easily imagine other plays for these companies continuing in the manner of Peele and persevering in the use of tumbling measures until the end of the decade. Those who can just as easily imagine these measures being used by Shakespeare in a play written for the Chamberlain's Men in the mid-nineties should come to the assistance of the stubborn-minded. Chambers suggests that he was "experimenting" with their comic effect in *The Comedy of Errors*.[18] Was he still "experimenting" in 1595? Charlton's explanation does not strike me as helpful. In dismissing the doggerel as indication of an early date, he says "it is somewhat as if Shakespeare's metrical level at the period of *Hamlet* should be judged by reckoning the Player's declamation and the play within the play as the normal type."[19] But this is precisely my point. The tumbling measures in *Love's Labor's Lost* appear in no extraneous portions of the play, but in exactly those portions where we should expect to find verse of the "normal type."

My second question has to do with why Shakespeare should perversely have hit upon such a constellation of character-names as "Navarre," "Berowne," "Longaville," and "Dumaine" for the members of his whimsical semi-Arcadian "academe" if the selection was made at any time later than August 1589. Before that date the choice was logical enough. The family of Navarre ruled in a small kingdom pleasingly associated in English minds with continental Protestantism, and the other names belonged to French noble houses important enough to be linked fictitiously with the "King of Navarre" in some never-never time when his name was Ferdinand, son of Charles. But after August, 1589, the case was different. By edict of the deceased Henry III, the actual "Navarre" was now King of France, engaged in a death-struggle with the League. The struggle was of crucial concern to the English. Three thousand English levies from London died in Navarre's cause in its first year. In 1591 the Earl of Essex was sent to assist him by besieging Rouen. In April of that year Essex banquetted with Navarre, Biron, and Longaville. The latter two were no longer just any French lords, but Navarre's most important generals. "Dumaine," in contrast, unless audiences had exercised heroic self-discipline in thought control, would have suggested du Maine or de Mayenne, brother of the Guise, and Navarre's formidable opponent. Then in July 1593 Navarre mightily offended Elizabeth and her nation by turning his religious coat and buying Paris "for a mass." It has been argued that such events made Shakespeare's character names "topical."[20] Rather they made the names a-topical or contra-topical. The author had been unlucky in his choice. Tucker Brooke has put the matter best:

> Doubtless Shakespeare first devised his fiction of Navarre and France at a period when it was possible to weave into it recent names and incidents [i.e. involving French embassies to Navarre in 1578-86] still too vague in their connotation for English auditors to

jar against the playful spirit of the comedy . . . [but]
to say nothing (virtually) of the military fame of the
four gentlemen and associate Dumaine in friendship
with the rest, or alternatively to confuse Dumaine
with d'Aumont, would have affronted common intelligence if attempted very long after the death of
Henry III (Aug. 2, 1589) had brought them all upon
the centre of the political stage.[21]

It is hard to believe that *Love's Labor's Lost* could have
been written or even performed in England between
August 1589 and July 1593, or that its character names
would have been voluntarily chosen between 1593 and
1598. Toward the end of the latter period they could
have been tolerated in a revival. They were worked into
the metrical pattern of a number of lines and would
have been hard to excise. Besides, luck was running
again with the author. After 1595 Navarre somewhat
rehabilitated his name by making war on Spain and
aligning himself again with the English. He and du
Maine ceased to be enemies. But there would still have
been small motive for associating four such portentous
names in scenes of pastoral jollity even in 1596-98—and
in referring only to a "war" in which Navarre had as-
sisted the "King of France" and incurred certain ex-
penses.

Some of those who have dated the original version of
the play in the mid-nineties have been a little discom-
fited by the facts just reviewed. Dover Wilson admits
the curious fact that in Shakespeare's play there is not
the "slightest reference" to the war, and surmises that
"in 1593 Shakespeare had worked over the manuscript
of a 'French comedy' dealing with the incidents referred
to [i.e. those of the 1578 French embassy to Navarre]

and originally plotted by another dramatist somewhere in the 'eighties."[22] This does not make quite clear whether the "French comedy" envisioned was a comedy in French or a comedy about France. If the first is intended, I know of no school of French drama of the time which discussed the affairs of the contemporary *haut monde*, using the names of actual lords. If the second is intended, I see no reason why it should have been "originally plotted by another dramatist" rather than Shakespeare himself. In any case "somewhere in the 'eighties" is something of a concession.

An elusive "French comedy" reappears in some curious remarks by W. W. Greg:

> Such adumbration of contemporary characters, particularly in an amiable light, is not exactly what we should expect after Henri IV had forfeited English sympathy by turning Catholic in the summer of 1593, and there are references in the play that point to a date later than this. It is possible, therefore, that Shakespeare worked on the basis of an earlier 'French comedy' that drew upon sources not generally available; but even if that was the case, there is no necessity to suppose that he took from it more than the general situation together with a few names and incidental allusions.[23]

The phrase "not exactly what we should expect" strikes me as an understatement, and unless there are inferences in the passage that escape me, its end contradicts its beginning. Shakespeare, using a "French comedy," voluntarily selected from it those very names the involuntary selection of which the French comedy was originally hypothesized to explain. It seems to me simpler to suppose that he wrote his play about 1588-89 when the selection of the names was logical, and revised it about 1596-97 when the retention of the names was permissable.

My final question is, why should a play written for adult professionals in the mid-nineties so much resemble plays written for child professionals in the mid-eighties? The resemblance is not superficial. It is observable in content, form, and spirit. It seems highly suggestive that all the basic ingredients of the play became available in a cluster in the decade before 1588, and nothing that became available thereafter was used except incidental phrases. Although I agree with many students of the play, that the Holofernes-Nathaniel dialogues belong to the revision, my present point does not hinge upon this assumption.

This is no place to discuss in detail the "sources" of *Love's Labor's Lost*. Its central situation bears some relation to an actual visit in 1578 to Henry of Navarre at Nérac by Marguerite de Valois and her mother, Catherine of France. The royal visitors were accompanied by *l'escadron volant* of ladies in waiting, and Aquitaine was discussed as part of Marguerite's dowry. (The parallels with Shakespeare's play were first noted in a good article by John Phelps in 1899[24] and not, as invariably stated, in a bad book by Abel Lefranc in 1919.) The negotiations were of a kind to provoke continental gossip, which seems to have reached the ears of Shakespeare, but they were not epoch-making, and the interest in the gossip would not long have survived the more spectacular relations between France and Navarre of 1589 and later. By 1595 such gossip would have been very "old hat." The idea of a Gallic contemplative retreat (associated with Anjou rather than Navarre) appears in de la Primaudaye's *French Academy,* translated into English in 1586. The stock characters of *commedia dell'arte,* which seem to have influenced the conception of Armado and Moth, not to speak of Holofernes and Nathaniel, became known to the English through visits of Italian troupes to London before 1588.[25] The plays of Lyly whose specific influence is discernible in *Love's Labor's Lost* were written between 1584 and 1588. Lyly enthusiasts may have overstated the indebtedness, but it remains true that in *Campaspe* there is an incipient philosophical "academy" and a conflict between love and kingly resolves. (In fact the claim of military austerity, or of friendship, or of philosophical detachment as opposed to the claim of love between the sexes was a staple theme of the early "courtesy books" as well as of the chorister drama for genteel audiences.) In *Gallathea* (III.i) Diana's nymphs successively confess their broken vows and agree collectively to succumb to passion; there is certainly some influence here upon the progressive revelations of recusancy in the most famous scene (IV.iii) in *Love's Labor's Lost*. In *Endymion* the Sir Tophas-Epiton-Bagoa triad shows more than an accidental resemblance to the Armado-Moth-Jacquenetta triad in *Love's Labor's Lost*. It would be phenomenal if so many reminiscences of Lyly in Shakespeare were a delayed manifestation of 1595. And, finally, the one plot ingredient that has been supposed conclusively to indicate a late date[26] indicates nothing of the kind. The Gray's Inn revels of 1594, in which there was a *conjunction* of Muscovite maskers and blackamoor torch-bearers, has been strongly urged as a source of Shakespeare's play. But there was just this conjunction in an actual court masque of 1510, and, more important, this masque was described in one of Shakespeare's favorite books, *Holinshed's Chronicles*, 1587.[27] Combined with the actual visit of ludicrous Russians to Elizabeth's court in 1583, this would have been suggestion enough; and although the Gray's Inn revellers may have hit upon the device independently, they may also have remembered it in *Love's Labor's Lost*: they are as likely to have been Shakespeare's debtors as his creditors.

The structure of *Love's Labor's Lost* is radically different from that of typical Shakespearean comedy, and the difference is in the direction of Chapel and Paul's drama of the eighties—in the grouping and balancing of characters, the at-least-perfunctory deference to the "unities," the fairly equitable distribution of lines among the characters, the emphasis upon words at the expense of action, the use of scenes as set pieces rather than as links in an integrated plot. One must note also the large number of parts calling for non-adult actors (five women and a boy), and the absence of a professional court jester even in a comic court. So far as the spirit of the piece is concerned, one hesitates to be frank in the teeth of all that has been said about its adult suavity. It has been praised as representing the very acme of courtly grace, genteel manners, and sophisticated wit, but a reasonably objective reading, with attention to what the characters are actually saying, somewhat shakes one's faith. It is all in good fun, true enough, but the manners projected are atrocious and the characters uniformly barbarous. Their repartee consists largely in attacks upon each other's morals, intelligence, and personal appearance. When not reviling each other, they are reviling each other's sweethearts, whose complexions suggest to the speakers pockiness, dirt, shoe-leather, and other unsavory similes. Some of the retorts are brutal, and they by no means "abrogate scurrility." The one character whose manners achieve a minimal level of social decency is none other than the main butt of the piece—gentle Don Armado. The comic effect derives in the main from impudence, pertness and animal spirits. In their offstage moments the "king" and his lords are visualized as tumbling about like frolicsome kids.[28] The atmosphere of boisterous juvenility is not a characteristic shared with the plays of Lyly, which are usually quite decorous, but it appears in chorister drama of a later period. I find it more congenial to imagine *Love's Labor's Lost* originally in the repertory of boy actors rather than of grown men.

That the play may have been written for children has been several times suggested,[29] but there has been a singular reluctance to follow the idea home to its logical conclusion. A play originally written for boys would, we should suppose, originally have been produced by a chorister company in a "private" theatre if such a theatre were operating at the time when the play was written. But even those who have vigorously urged 1588-89 as the date of original composition, for instance F. G. Fleay and latterly T. W. Baldwin, have stopped short of such a suggestion. Although Professor Baldwin claims too much for the idea of its only-rudimentary adherence to the alleged "five-act structure" as an indication of early date, and concedes too little about the late style and verbal allusions in parts of the play, nevertheless his defence of his dating is often cogent.[30] The trouble is that, like Fleay, he claims the play for Strange's Men playing at the Cross Keys, and it is hard to think of *Love's Labor's Lost* in any form being produced at a converted inn as a rival attraction with a performing horse. None of the popular plays of the eighties resemble it in the least. A decade later, revised, somewhat humanized, and equipped with the sure-fire Holofernes and Nathaniel, it might have gone over as a novelty with a popular audience. Shakespeare himself had helped to educate such audiences in word-play: "We must speak by the card, or equivocation will undo us. By the Lord, Horatio, this three years I have taken note of it, the age is grown so picked that the toe of the peasant comes so near the heel of the courtier he galls his kibe." Still, we must remember that the play is never listed with his popular hits in its own time, and the only specifically indicated performances are those before Queen Elizabeth and Queen Anne.[31]

In 1588-89 there were facilities for such a play as *Love's Labor's Lost* in the commercial theatre of London. Although the Chapel Children had lost the first Blackfriars in 1584, they retained at least a shadowy existence. We hear of them on tour at Norwich in 1586-87 and at Leicester in 1590-91.[32] In 1594 two plays were published with identical inscriptions, "Played by the children of her Maiesties Chappell."[33] Although both seem considerably earlier than the year of publication, both contain writing later than 1584 when the Blackfriars ceased operating. However, the Paul's theatre provides the more interesting possibility. This remained open until 1590, generating plays which were good enough for occasional selection for performance at court. All we have of what must have been an extensive repertory is a few plays by John Lyly. We know positively that there were other plays and other playwrights. Let me propose that Shakespeare's *Love's Labor's Lost* in its original form was written for Paul's in 1588-89 and see what the hypothesis suggests.

The abruptness with which unmistakable allusions to Shakespeare in London begin to appear in 1590-93 creates the impression that his presence there, as distinct from the allusions, was also abrupt. Chambers seems to predicate a swift translation from Stratford to London in 1590, and an equally swift transformation of a provincial artisan or idler of twenty-six into an actor and playwright. In view of the general paucity of allusions to particular companies, plays, and playwrights in and before the period in question, the evidence will bear no such construction, and the probabilities are against it. Neither, in view of the circumstances, does the allusion to him as an "upstart crow" mean that he was *really* an upstart; and we know definitely that the work he himself called the "first heir" of his invention was not *really* the first. Those who predicate for him an earlier career in the theatre try to trace back the ancestry of the Chamberlain's and Strange's companies and then postulate his association with such shadowy combinations of actors as emerge. This is better, but also vulnerable, since there was always much recruiting as well as realignment among acting groups. We do not know how Shakespeare became an actor: he may have joined a country troupe after he reached his majority;

he may have come to London and haunted the theatres; he may have become a chapel boy in the household of a lord and been superannuated into the theatre. In 1582 Stephen Gosson speaks of actors "trained up from their childhood in this abominable exercise,"[34] and there is no lack of later evidence of chapel actors graduating into adult companies. As Hamlet says of the little eyases, "Will they not say afterwards if they should grow themselves to common players (as it is most like, if their means are no better), their writers do them wrong to make them exclaim against their own succession?" That Shakespeare himself may have walked this route has long been recognized as possible. We know that he was born in 1564, that he married and became a father in 1582-83, and that his wife bore him twins in Stratford in 1585. But marrying and even begetting twins are not exclusive occupations. His residence in Stratford from childhood may have been intermittent, and he may have been selected as a chapel child, as the gifted sons of plain people frequently were. It is not only the period between his production of twin children in Stratford in 1585 and his production of twin plays in London in 1590-91 that must be designated the "lost years."

As a chapel child, dwelling part of the time in a great house, part of the time behind his father's shop, Shakespeare would have gained that insight into two worlds which is one of his most striking characteristics. He would have continued with the education in Latin begun in the Stratford grammar school. As a youth he might have taught younger chapel boys, and guided them in the performance of plays. I wish now to bring together some scattered data which have never been satisfactorily explained and which may have some bearing on our subject. The solitary item in the "Shakespeare mythos" which scholars have been inclined to take seriously is John Aubrey's jotting, "He understood Latin pretty well: for he had been in his younger yeares a School-master in the Countrey."[35] There are several reasons for taking it seriously: the information came from Beeston, the son of a member of Shakespeare's own acting company; there is nothing scandalous about it such as would have appealed to Aubrey; there is nothing "generic" about it like the stories of deer-poaching and the like; and finally there is nothing in the least striking or colorful about it such as would suggest any reason for communicating it except the fact that it was true.

Now what does "School-master in the Countrey" suggest? To the American it suggests "country schoolmaster," perhaps evoking the image of Ichabod Crane. To the English I suspect that it suggests Nickleby's term of servitude in Dotheboys Hall, and perhaps the reference to the "charge-house on the top of the mountain" (V.i.58) where Holofernes presides would fortify this impression. I am ignorant of the various routes to the teaching profession in the sixteenth century, but I am inclined to believe that a regular "schoolmaster" would normally be a university graduate, and that the equivalent of an usher would only be found in a sizable school in a sizable town. My guess is that "in the Countrey" as Beeston or Aubrey would use the term would mean "in a country house"—the seat of a landed gentleman or nobleman. Here a non-university youth might

quite well pass on such Latin as he had acquired to the
more youthful recruits of the chapel, taking this load
off the chaplain.

Chapels in the environs of London transformed themselves into regular acting companies, the occupants of
"private" theatres. Chapels "in the country" sometimes
went on theatrical tours. The "Earl of Oxford's Company" played at Bristol in 1581, "being I man and IX
boys."[36] In 1581 Shakespeare was seventeen, "a codling
when 'tis almost an apple: 'tis with him in standing
water, between man and boy"; hence we might cast him
either as the "I man" or one of the "IX boys" and remember that an association with Oxford's chapel could have
landed him in 1584 squarely in the first Blackfriars
theatre—as a coach and writer, of course, rather than as
a juvenile actor. We may write off Oxford entirely (bale-
ful name in Shakespearean speculation) and still recognize that Shakespeare may have penetrated the acting
profession by almost growing up in it. We must always
recognize that such an unusual man must have been an
unusual boy and youth, and that there were "divers of
worship" other than Oxford who could have brought
him into the orbit of the Blackfriars and Paul's theatricals. With F. P. Wilson I fully agree that he must have
known he was a poet from the first. I should go further
and say that anyone who wrote plays like his of the early
nineties, inferior though they may be when compared to
his own later work, had nevertheless been writing plays
for a considerable length of time.

Shakespeare lacked the family connections and the
university degree of a John Lyly, such as might have put
him in charge of a chapel company, but he could have

served as a "Johannes factotum." Chapel masters had at one time acted with their boys, and occasional rôles in the plays of Lyly, such as that of Sir Tophas, suggest that the tradition of including an adult actor may have been maintained. Perhaps an adult who had been a chapel-boy actor would have been a useful adjunct about Paul's when long commercialization had rendered acting *infra dig* for the chapel master or the genteel entrepreneur associated with him. A good adult voice may have been useful too—and a good composer of songs. This brings me to a second of the unsolved puzzles about the drama of the time. Who wrote the songs for Lyly's plays, nearly all of which were excluded from editions during Lyly's lifetime? W. W. Greg's argument that Lyly did not write them is better than his argument that Dekker did.[37] Some of them are not only worthy of Shakespeare, but are as much in his vein as in Dekker's, notably Appeles' song and Trico's song (V.i) in *Campaspe*. The latter reminds us of the concluding songs in *Love's Labor's Lost,* and contains phrases either repeated in or plagiarized from Shakespeare's own "Hark, hark, the lark."

The final unsolved puzzle I wish to mention is one of the strangest in our early dramatic history. Who was the subject of Spenser's lines in the lament of Thalia in *The Teares of the Muses,* registered in 1590 and printed in 1591 in *Complaints*?

> And he the man, whom Nature selfe had made
> To mock her selfe, and Truth to imitate,
> With kindly counter vnder Mimick shade,
> Our pleasant *Willy*, an is dead of late:
> With whom all ioy and iolly meriment
> Is also deaded, and in dolour drent.

In stead therof scoffing Scurrilitie,
And scornfull Follie with Contempt is crept,
Rolling in rymes of shameles ribaudrie
Without regard, or due Decorum kept,
Each idle wit at will presumes to make,
And doth the Learneds task vpon him take.

But that same gentle Spirit, from whose pen
Large streames of honnie and sweete Nectar flowe,
Scorning the boldnes of such base-borne men,
Which dare their follies forth so rashlie throwe;
Doth rather choose to sit in idle Cell,
Than so himself to mockerie to sell.[38]

If Shakespeare suddenly appeared in the rôle of playwright in 1590, of course the lines could not refer to
him. If he had been writing long enough for an interval
to have occurred in his output just before 1590, the case
is quite different. It is easy to say that Shakespeare was
not the subject of the lines, but it is almost as easy to
say that *no one* was the subject of the lines; it is impossible to name anyone writing joyous poetic comedy
before 1590 with talent enough to command Spenser's
respect. But there the lines stand, demanding an explanation; such comedies must have been written, or Thalia
would have had nothing to lament. After canvassing the
field, Chambers happily rejects his own suggestion of
Dick Tarlton, then, in fault of better, hits upon John
Lyly. But the lines do not suggest the literary personality
of John Lyly, and Lyly was not inactive as a playwright
in 1589-90; in fact he was involved in the Marprelate
controversy; and it was the "scoffing Scurrilitie" and
"shameles ribaudrie" of the plays of this controversy
which led to the closing of Paul's and presumably to
Thalia's lament. It is easy enough to guess what spate

of comedies Spenser deplored; the difficulty lies in guessing what kindly comedies preceded them.

I am led to two reflections: first, that if anyone in his times was equipped to recognize Shakespeare's talents promptly, and to recognize their essential quality, it was Edmund Spenser; and second, that if Spenser's lines really did refer to Shakespeare, it would be the irony of the ages that the fact remains unconceded. After detecting allusions to Shakespeare in every likely and unlikely place, we would have failed to detect one in "our pleasant Willy . . . that same gentle Spirit." The idea of Shakespeare as the source of "streams of honnie and sweet Nectar" furnishes the first critical *cliché* that appears in authenticated allusions to his writing; and the idea of Shakespeare as one "whom Nature selfe had made To mock herself, and Truth to imitate" (i.e. that he was as true to nature as nature herself) furnishes the second critical *cliché* and the one which endured for a century and a half. Perhaps it is just too obvious to be believed.

No one in his right mind would wish to associate Shakespeare with the coterie theatres rather than the popular theatres, which produced the best drama of the era and where he obviously realized himself. But an apprenticeship in the coterie theatres would not have been disabling; players destined for the big leagues often begin in the little leagues. No one, either, would wish to part scholarly company with such men as E. K. Chambers, G. L. Kittredge, W. W. Greg, and F. P. Wilson in order to link arms with Furnivall and Fleay. Our twentieth-century "paragons of caution" have performed a great service in resisting "disintegration," super-subtle theories about ur-texts, progressive revision and the like. They have assumed, reasonably, that the existing texts of plays are the "original" texts or at least the ones most worth dating and discussing. But occasionally these scholars, useful though their stalwart skepticism has been, may have overstated their cases; and in their anxiety to shore up the wind-racked structure of Shakespearean scholarship, they may have boarded up certain doors.

I have proved nothing in this article, but I hope I have indicated why I should be sorry if the opinion that *Love's Labor's Lost* was first written in the mid-nineties should inexorably "harden into an orthodoxy." I think that this play is more likely than any other to suggest the avenues of investigation if there is ever to be a "break-through" in our knowledge of Shakespeare's theatrical beginnings. If I may resort once more to the jargon of our technological age, it is the only play, with the possible exception of the *Comedy of Errors*, [39] which contains "built-in" evidence of a date before 1590, along with hints of the original auspices of production.

FOOTNOTES

[1] F. P. Wilson, *Marlowe and the Early Shakespeare* (Oxford, 1953), p. 113. The author on p. 121 passingly refers to *Love's Labor's Lost* as coming "soon" after the early plays and parodying their "artifices of style."
[2] H. H. Furness, *New Variorum Edition* (1904), p. 337, quoting William Winter (1891).
[3] *Life of Shakespeare* (London, 1898), p. 50. The statement remains unchanged in subsequent editions; cf. ed. 1917, p. 102, and others.
[4] *Shakespeare: Complete Works* (1936), p. 193.
[5] *William Shakespeare, A Study of Facts and Problems* (Oxford, 1933), I, 338.
[6] New Cambridge Edition (1923), p. xxxiv.
[7] New Arden Edition (1951), p. 1.

[8] Letter of Sir Walter Cope to Robert Cecil, Lord Cranborne, endorsed "1604" apparently for January 1605; cf. Chambers, II, p. 332. (I am assuming that the letter refers to the performance noted in Chambers, II, p. 331.)

[9] *Henslowe's Diary*, ed. W. W. Greg (London, 1904-08), I, p. 116.

[10] This is the view of W. W. Greg, *The Shakespeare First Folio* (Oxford 1955), pp. 219-223.

[11] *The Satirical Comedy, Love's Labor's Lost* (New York, 1933).

[12] *Sous le masque de William Shakespeare* (Paris, 1918-19), II, pp. 87-100.

[13] The most conspicuous modern works on the "topicalities" since the speculations of F. G. Fleay, Arthur Acheson, and J. M. Robertson have been: Austin K. Gray, "The Secret of *Love's Labour's Lost," PMLA*, XXXIX (1924), 581-611; John Dover Wilson, *Love's Labour's Lost*, New Cambridge Shakespeare (1923); Francis A. Yates, *A Study of Love's Labour's Lost* (Cambridge University Press ,1936); Muriel C. Bradbrook, *The School of Night* (Cambridge University Press, 1936). More conservative but bearing in the same direction is Rupert Taylor's *The Date of Love's Labour's Lost* (New York, 1932). A general endorsement seems to be given the speculative school by Richard David in his edition for the new Arden Shakespeare (1951).

[14] There are a few quite brief patches of doggerel in *Two Gentlemen of Verona* and *The Taming of the Shrew*; elsewhere in Shakespeare's acknowledged plays there is only a scattered couplet or two, serving a specific whimsical purpose.

[15] Allison Gaw, "The Evolution of the *Comedy of Errors," PMLA*, XLI (1926), pp. 620-666.

[16] *History of English Dramatic Literature* (London, 1875), I, p. 372.

[17] *History of English Poetry* (London, 1895-1910), IV (1903), p. 83.

[18] Chambers, I, p. 308.

[19] H. B. Charlton, "The Date of *Love's Labour's Lost," MLR*, XIII (1918), 17.

[20] *Ibid*. It does not follow that so good a scholar as H. B. Charlton still holds to views expressed in an article back in the times of the first world war.

[21] The Yale Shakespeare edition (1925), pp. 129, 134.

[22] New Cambridge Shakespeare, pp. 128, 130.

[23] *The Shakespeare First Folio*, p. 219.

[24] "The Source of Love's Labour's Lost," *Shakespeare Association Bulletin*, XVII (1942), 97-102. (This reprints from the *Baltimore Sun* the article of 1899; the author generously assumes that later publications represent independent discovery.) Other embassies to the court of Navarre have been mentioned as supplying suggestion, but none after 1586. Cf. Geoffrey Bullough, *Narrative and Dramatic Sources of Shakespeare*, I (London, 1957), pp. 425-442.

[25] O. J. Campbell, "*Love's Labour's Lost* Restudied," *Studies in Shakespeare, Milton and Donne. By members of the English Department of the University of Michigan* (1925). Professor Campbell's most telling points are that in the case of the *Capitano*, as Armado, the braggart is less a military swaggerer than a précieux; and that in the commedia dell'arte the *Affamato* (parasite) is attached to the *Dottore* (pedant) just as in *Love's Labor's Lost* Nathaniel is attached to Holofernes.

[26] Rupert Taylor, *op. cit.*, lays great emphasis on this "source."

[27] Fred Sorenssen, "The Masque of Muscovites in *Love's Labour's Lost*," *MLN*, L (1935), pp. 499-501.

[28] See the interesting passage, V.ii.90-118.

[29] See Campbell, p. 11; David, p. 1. Charles Knight in the introductory notice to the play in his *Pictorial Edition of the Works of Shakspere* (London, 1829-43) proposes that the play was written in 1589 when Shakespeare "was a joint proprietor in the Blackfriars theatre" (I, 76), but he seems, unfortunately, to have confused the second Blackfriars, acquired by the King's Men c. 1608, with the first Blackfriars, closed as a theatre in 1584.

[30] *Shakespeare's Five-Act Structure* (University of Illinois Press, 1947), p. 635.
[31] The second quarto, 1631, reprinting the play from the first folio "As it was acted by his Maiesties Seruants at the Blacke-Friers and the Globe" suggests a Caroline revival.
[32] J. T. Murray, *English Dramatic Companies* (London, 1910), I, p. 337.
[33] *The Wars of Cyrus*, and Marlowe and Nashe's *Tragedy of Dido*.
[34] *Plays Confuted in Five Actions* (1582), ed. W. C. Hazlitt, *English Drama and Stage* (London, 1869), p. 215.
[35] Chambers, II, p. 254.
[36] Murray, *English Dramatic Companies*, I, p. 345.
[37] "On the Authorship of the Songs in Lyly's Plays," *MLQ*, I (1905), 43-52. What appears to be a debased version of Trico's song printed in Dekker's *Sun's Darling* in 1656 is taken by Greg to be the "original" version of the song printed in Lyly's *Six Court Comedies* in 1632; I cannot follow the reasoning.
[38] Chambers, II, 186-187. Chambers also rejects as a reference to Shakespeare Spenser's lines in *Colin Clout's Come Home Again* (1591-95):

> And there though last not least is *Aetion*,
> A gentler shepheard may no where be found:
> Whose *Muse* full of high thoughts inuention,
> Doth like himselfe Heroically sound.

The last line suggests the heroic-sounding name "Shakespeare," and although Lee's ready acceptance of the identification seems a little uncritical, Chambers's ready rejection seems a little captious; the possibility remains open.
[39] I think the two plays should be studied in tandem. The *Comedy of Errors* may have originally been chorister-company Plautine "contamination" with intrigues multiplied in the fashion of Lyly's *Mother Bombie*, then later supplied with its humanizing frame. W. W. Greg observes that some of the stage directions suggest "a set stage with three houses" (*The Shakespeare First Folio*, p. 200). Such suggestion of a localized or scenic stage is a characteristic of all eleven texts of chorister drama before 1590, and *Love's Labor's Lost* itself could have been set "in pastoral" as could some of the plays of Lyly. The allusion in the *Comedy of Errors* to France "armed and reverted, making war against her heir" (III.ii.126) may belong to any time between August 1589 and July 1593, but signifies little if the text has been revised. A stronger link with *Love's Labor's Lost* is the fact that both texts share certain peculiarities and seem to have been set up from the same kind of copy. See Greg, p. 203 n.

Mavor Moore is a man whose life has been devoted to the worlds of literature and the theatre. He has directed plays, opera, revue, and radio and television productions and has acted in all media; his writings include articles for all the leading Canadian periodicals, several plays, and two musical comedies as well as innumerable items for *Spring Thaw* and a volume of verse, *And What Do You Do?*, published in 1960. From 1958 to 1961 he was Arts Editor of *Canadian Commentator* and he was for three years Drama, Opera, and Ballet Critic of *The Toronto Telegram*. He was a member of the original Board of Governors of the Stratford Festival. The study of witchcraft has been one of his major interests for many years and he has staged *Macbeth* three times, as well as *King Lear, The Tempest, A Midsummer Night's Dream,* and other plays involving magic: he has acted the part of Macbeth in two productions. His documentary *The Rise and Fall of Witchcraft* was broadcast by the CBC.

MAVOR MOORE

Shakespeare

and witchcraft

At the end of the play of *King Henry VIII*, Cranmer, the new Archbishop, makes a prophecy concerning the infant Elizabeth:

> "...   Let me speak, sir,
> For Heaven now bids me; and the words I utter
> Let none think flattery, for they'll find 'em truth.
> This royal infant—Heaven still move about her!—
> Though in her cradle, yet now promises
> Upon this land a thousand blessings..."

—and so on:

> "She shall be loved and feared: her own shall bless
>   her;
> Her foes shake like a field of beaten corn,
> And hang their heads with sorrow: good grows
>   with her.
> In her days every man shall eat in safety..."

"Thou speakest wonders," replies the flattered parent. Cranmer goes on:

> "She shall be, to the happiness of England,
> An aged princess; many days shall see her,
> And yet no day without a deed to crown it,
> Would I had known no more! but she must die,
> She must, the saints must have her, yet a virgin;

A most unspotted lily shall she pass
To the ground, and all the world shall mourn her."

This was the same Elizabeth who, 48 years later (in
1581), decreed a year's imprisonment and the pillory
for "any person (who) shall by casting of nativities or
by calculation or by any prophesying, witchcraft, con-
jurations . . . seek to know . . . how long her Majesty
shall live."

As the anthropologist Margaret Murray puts it:
"When divination is done in the name of the deity of
one of the established religions it is called prophecy;
when, however, divination is done in the name of a
pagan god it is mere witchcraft."

It is a curious fact that although Shakespeare lived at
the height of the witchcraft hysteria (it lasted for only
about 300 years, from 1450 to 1750), and although it
figures with some prominence in at least eleven of his
plays, in all the mountains of commentary there have
been few attempts to assess the significance of witchcraft
in his work—and even fewer based on historical fact
free of emotional, literary or religious prejudice. The
reason may be less curious. We have depended for our
ideas about witchcraft too often on the Christian historians, who were (to put it mildly) the most prejudiced
observers possible; recent archeological and anthropo-
logical studies are doing much to alter our views, but
seem hardly to have touched Shakespearean criticism,
let alone the popular image. It would be difficult to find,
in all the history of mankind, a more vivid example of
the successful "smear," for while scholars are not in complete agreement regarding details, and several

hypotheses still hold the field, it is now generally agreed that the Christian Church for centuries set out through its historians (and its near-monopoly of the printed record) to discredit a rival religion by making it appear an anti-religion. The Horned God of the pagan creeds— which existed in various forms from India to Scandinavia—was turned into the Christian Devil, horns, tail, cloven hoof and all; his worshippers (and especially his priests and priestesses) were transformed into demons; and the rituals attending his worship were translated from merely *non*-Christian into *anti*-Christian (and therefore anti-religious) blasphemy.

To turn things upside down in this way was not as difficult as it may sound; much of the paraphernalia of the old religion bore a natural resemblance to that of the new, and illiterate folk might easily be persuaded the father was a parody of his offspring. The ancient cauldron, for example, was clearly invented to mock the holy chalice; making oracles of cats and dogs was an intentional affront to those who saw God more often in a lamb; any cruciform, no matter how ancient, was demonstrably a parody of the crucifix; cannibalism and human sacrifice, even if extremely rare, were without a doubt mockeries of the mass, wherein Christians only *pretended* to eat and drink the body of Christ; and spells and sympathetic magic (that is, attempting to influence the course of nature by charms and acts simulating the desired effect) were naturally wicked inversions of such improved Christian models as holy water, divine relics, consecrated wafers, blessing, and the laying on of hands. To make matters worse, the worshippers of the ancient Horned God often elected to celebrate their rites without their clothes on, and shamelessly demonstrated their joy in heaven's bounty by dancing as well as singing. More than that: they moved in their dances from right to left—which is highly sinister.

Julius Caesar, for example, in his *De Bello Gallico,* tells us that Druidesses in Britain made rain by sprinkling water over nude virgins—a practice interpreted by Christian authorities as "baptism" into heathenism.

The "heathen" were, of course, merely the "people of the heath," the stubborn adherents of the old religion outside the more Christianized towns and cities. The *Encyclopedia Britannica* says: "When examining the records of the medieval witches, we are dealing with the remains of a pagan religion which survived, in England, at least, till the eighteenth century, 1200 years after the introduction of Christianity. . . . As civilization increased and Christianity became more firmly rooted, the old religion retreated to the less frequented parts of the country and was practised by the more ignorant members of the community." We do not need to swallow all the more exotic theories advanced by Dr. Margaret Murray, the *Britannica's* authority on witchcraft, to accept this reasonable premise, supported as it is by most modern authorities and particularly by Gerald Gardner, an anthropologist who lives and works among survivors of the ancient cult in the Isle of Man. A new religion cannot replace an old one overnight. And as Robbins tells us in his recent *Encyclopedia of Witchcraft and Demonology* (where he puts Dr. Murray in her place as forthrightly as anyone), for 13 centuries after the founding of the Church its leaders were remarkably tolerant of the continuance of old pagan practices, expecting no doubt that time and reason would make the superstitious see the light. During that whole era, official heresy consisted not in practising witchcraft so much as in believing it would work. As Horace had written long ago (the translation is Elizabethan):

> "These dreams and terrors magicall,
> These miracles and witches,
> Night-walking sprites, or Thessal bugs,
> Esteem them not two rushes."

And then about the middle of the fifteenth century the Church, like a tolerant father losing his patience, declared all-out war on its tenacious theological rival; the Inquisition was on, with no holds barred. The Catholic jurist Jean Bodin wrote:

> "Wherefore it is that one accused of being a witch ought never to be fully acquitted and set free . . . inasmuch as the proof of such crimes is so obscure and difficult that not one witch in a million would be accused or punished if the procedure were governed by the ordinary rules."

Nor did it help the witches that by the practice of their old rites they often performed beneficial feats. Here speaks the Calvinist theologian, William Perkins:

> "Though the witch were in many respects profitable, and did not hurt but procured much good, yet, because he hath renounced God his king and governor and bound himself by other laws to the service of the enemies of God and his church, death is his portion justly assigned to him by God: he may not live."

(Incidentally, God said no such thing: the Bible quotation "Thou shalt not suffer a witch to live," is in fact a mistranslation; the original refers to "a poisoner," which seems fair enough.) At a conservative estimate over 200,000 supposed witches were put to death during the witch hunt between the fifteenth and eighteenth centuries, and many times that number hideously tortured, all in the name of the Christian Church whose records we have accepted as history.

In the flood-tide of this nemesis, of course, were caught many who were not witches at all, in any sense of the word, but merely victims of social or personal spite; and one of the difficulties we face in unravelling our ideas about witches is that the confessions of these unfortunates, elicited under appalling torture, self-contradictory and often nonsensical, have come to be believed. They were ready to confess anything, especially whatever horrors and horrid delights their captors wished to hear told of, including orgiastic sabbaths, flying, infanticide, and blood-signed contracts with Satan. The legal definition of a witch was "One who, knowing God's law, tries to bring about some act through an agreement with the devil" (Bodin); not only the deed but the mere intention was punishable, and the crime might therefore be entirely imaginary and still be punishable. It is on these grounds that Robbins denies there ever was such a thing as a "witch," and in terms of the legal definition then applied he may be right. But the people *accused* of witchcraft were unquestionably real, and many of these, however confused their "confessions," apparently died as martyrs to a faith that claimed their devotion even unto death by hanging or roasting. If they were not, or could not have been, "witches" in the legal fiction, they almost certainly were adherents of the old faith, the destruction of which was the Church's prime and initial concern. A further reason that we have been unwilling to examine this era closely may be that we are always less than eager to dwell on the ugly subject of mass torture and persecution, just as we now shy away from reliving the Nazi pogrom of the last world war.

But Shakespeare did not have to relive it; he lived through it. And it seems to me incredible that a man of his extraordinary sensitivity should have been unaware of the mass injustice being practised, when around him were sceptics such as Francis Bacon or Florio, who believed professed witches to be mere human if deluded beings, or such as the Catholic priest who wrote in 1592:

> "O Christian religion, how long shalt thou be vexed with this direst of superstitions? . . . O Christian commonwealth, how long in thee shall the life of the innocent be imperilled?"

This is no place for a history of witchcraft (see Robbins' *Encyclopedia*) or a dissertation on its theology (see Gardner's *Witchcraft Today*); but we must, before proceeding to Shakespeare's plays, recognize at least that for centuries witchcraft was purposely (let alone accidentally) confused with sorcery, occultism, and demonology in an attempt to discredit the old religion, that we cannot believe the highly imaginative ravings under torture of poor wretches whose only crime may have been the possession of a house the in-

quisitor coveted, that witches, whatever impossibilities
they professed, were real human beings, and that the
very vehemence of the purge instituted by both Catholic
and Protestant authorities (each often blaming the other
for the continuing prevalence of superstition) stands as
a monument to the enduring stubbornness of an earlier
faith.

Further than this, there is plenty of evidence that
even when a veneer of Christian precept and practice
was adopted for safety's sake, most of the common folk
and even some of the gentry and nobility continued to
honour the ancient beliefs and customs. In 1282 the
priest of Inverkeithing had led the fertility dance around
his own churchyard; as late as the seventeenth century
the apprentices of York danced in the Minster itself; and
in 1661, even, Madame Bourignon was able to report
from Lille that:

> "No assemblies were ever seen so numerous in the
> City as in these Sabbaths, where came people of all
> qualities and conditions—young and old, rich and
> poor, noble and ignoble, but especially all sorts of
> monks and nuns, priests and prelates."

And that, let us remind ourselves, was in the fearsome
face of the still vigorous and unscrupulous Inquisition.

Worshippers of the most primitive sort, of course, had
long since betaken themselves where they might live in
peace in their old ways, little changed from the Stone
Age. These were probably the original inhabitants of
Britain, or such early-comers as the Picts (from whom
we surely derive our word "pixies"). "They live in wilds
and forests and on mountains," Waldron tells us in his
Isle of Man, "and shun great cities because of the

wickedness acted therein." They adhered to their
ancient dress and customs, occasionally sallying forth
to steal food or wives, attacking their enemies with
poisoned arrows, and thus giving rise to the tales about
"fairies." Modern discoveries of their relics, homes, and
artifacts, have established their actuality, yet even some
scholars today seem unaware that the fairies were real.
Elizabethans laboured under no such delusion. Dr. Elizabeth Latham, in her book *The Elizabethan Fairies*, says
unequivocally:

> "In most of the references to the fairies in the 16th
> century they are treated as real and existing en-
> tities."

Bovet, in his *Pandaemonium* (1684) tells of an actual
fairyland:

> "Those that have had occasion to travel that way
> have frequently seen them there, appearing like
> men and women of a stature generally nearer the
> size of smaller men; their habits used to be of red,
> blue or green, according to the old way of country
> garb, with high-crowned hats . . ."

We cannot here go into the differences, however marked,
between the fairies and the witches; suffice it to say
that both adhered to the old religion of the Horned
God, and that some fairies who lived openly among the
villagers would become known as witches. Often the
words are used interchangeably, in this sense, by the
Elizabethans, and so I may be pardoned for doing so
in this context. I shall try not to take advantage of the
ambiguity. In any case, the descendants of these people
are still to be noted in Britain, particularly in districts
off the beaten track, such as the Isle of Man, where

Gerald Gardner has joined and witnessed their ceremonies, some of which are traditionally descended from
pre-Roman Britain.

That Shakespeare was familiar with their existence
and way of life is more than apparent. Dr. Latham
states:

> "Had every source of information been lost concern-
> ing the fairies of the period, all the characteristic
> features of their world and most of the ceremonies
> consequent on its existence could have been repro-
> duced from his writings."

And that he accepted them as real beings is evident
from both *The Merry Wives of Windsor* and *Pericles,*
where humans are quite rationally mistaken for fairies.

His treatment of the pagan world and pagan characters, moreover, never slights their reality or their humanity. In *King Lear* he writes entirely of a pagan society,
and in this play (unless I am mistaken) undertakes the
huge and usually unrecognized task of putting the whole
corpus of the old religion, with its belief in power over
the elements through ritual magic, through the spectro-
scope of Christian dogma. In the Roman plays he de-
lineates with rare care, for his day, the Mediterranean
religion which later coloured (if ever so slightly) that
of the Britons it tried to subdue. In *Cymbeline,* with its
queen "who brews poison out of innocent violets, cow-
slips, and primroses," he matches the worlds of ancient
Britain and ancient Rome. ("Britain," Pliny the Elder
tells us, "might have taught magic to Persia." And from
Geoffrey of Monmouth we learn that Lear's father, King
Bladud, "was a right cunning craftsman, and did teach

nigromancy throughout the realm of Britain.") In *Macbeth* he crashes together—among other things; I do not wish to suggest this as a monopolistic exegesis—the witchmonger Macbeths and the Christianized nobility of the more civilized English court. In Glendower and Prospero we meet two professional magicians who are treated with serious consideration as human beings, however diverse Shakespeare's attitude toward their magical power.

I wish time permitted us to follow all of these excursions into the realm of fairies and witches, and even more keenly do I wish I might dwell on two other plays: *King Henry VI,* in which Shakespeare's version of Joan of Arc as a witch makes more and greater sense as historians become increasingly convinced that Joan was in reality the high-priestess of the old religion in France, and a Christian saint only on the premise that what you can't lick you must join, and *A Midsummer Night's Dream,* in which Shakespeare mysteriously elected, single-handed, to alter the whole tradition of the English fairy; how well he did it is shown by popular unwillingness nowadays to believe the fairies were, until his time, anything else. Writes Dr. Latham:

> "Before 1594 and *A Midsummer Night's Dream,* as far as can be ascertained, there is no record of any diminutive fairies or elves in the 16th century in England."

And again:

> "In all pages of their record, with the exception of the fairies of Shakespeare's mythology, and the fairies of Spenser, the fairies as a race are never referred to as *good* spirits, except when this adjective is applied to them as a matter of propitiation and fear."

And a whole book could be written about how and why Shakespeare takes "Robin Goodfellow," one version of the unspeakable name of the god incarnate of the old religion, and thus to Christians a senior demon, and turns him into the merry sprite, Puck. It surely cannot have been unintentional, for Shakespeare evidently knew the territory.

All this suggests that the great A. C. Bradley was postulating wildly when he wrote of Macbeth:

> "Of course in the popular notion the witches' spirits are devils or servants of Satan. If Shakespeare openly introduces this idea only in such phrases as 'the instruments of darkness' and 'what! can the devil speak true?' the reason is probably his unwillingness to give too much prominence to distinctively religious ideas."

I suggest that his willingness to give prominence to distinctively religious ideas is everywhere apparent, and that we have rather been slow to appreciate it because we have, until very recently, not known or acknowledged enough about the older faith which was so much a part of his religious environment.

I propose, therefore, to examine *Macbeth,* in such detail as time permits, with a view to inspiring others to re-examine other works in a similar light.

II

As few editors fail to inform us, King James of Scotland was already a notable demonologist and witchhunter when he transferred his court to England three years before *Macbeth* was first produced. It is generally

agreed that this play concerning witches, an earlier King
of Scotland, the new queen's forebear, Lady Glamis, and
James' own progenitor, Banquo, was written especially
for the new court. "The accession of James, who had a
passion for burning old women alive," notes Dover
Wilson, "made witches the great question of that age."
But Wilson, in common with most editors and commen-
tators, goes on to answer that question by putting words
into Shakespeare's mouth—or at any rate elaborating
with alarming abandon:

> "*Macbeth* is a first-rate shocker . . . The play opens
> with a vision of foul hags grinning and capering in
> obscene dances, hovering through the fog and filthy
> air."

Or, as it is put in the Stevenson text, generally used in
our Ontario public and high schools:

> "In the opening scene of the play of *Macbeth*, the
> curtain rises upon a desert place, with thunder and
> lightning." [*Shakespeare's text, incidentally,
> speaks of no such "desert place"—it is a gratuitous
> early gloss: Dr. Forman's contemporary description
> of the play says Macbeth and Banquo met the
> women "ridinge thorowe a wod."*]

> "Imagine, as you read the scene, the dress and ex-
> pression of these malignant creatures, their uncanny
> movements, gestures and tones of voice, accom-
> panied as they were by thunder and lightning,
> and you may form some idea of how their appear-
> ance might affect superstitious people." [*Whether
> the Elizabethans were much more superstitious
> than we, with our horoscopes, extra-sensory percep-
> tion—"CAN WE KNOW THE FUTURE?" screams
> a headline in today's paper—and pseudo-scientific
> fads, seems to me a moot point.*] "These witches

are not creatures of good omen, for we know that their associates are cats, toads, and other repulsive creatures; and they tell us that what is fair and good to other people is foul and evil to them, and they 'hover through the fog and filthy air'."

We shall return to these inaccurate, incredibly snobbish denigrations in a moment; but first two other claims in the Stevenson text must be dealt with.

"In Shakespeare's time the belief in witches was widespread; and the Weird Sisters in *Macbeth* have all the qualities which were usually associated with the witches of popular superstition." [*If the popular attitude then was one of superstition, why does the editor's attitude, as shown above, follow suit?*] "But [they] are something more than the witches of vulgar superstition. They are the Weird Sisters . . . 'the spirits that know all mortal consequences' . . . 'they have more in them than mortal knowledge'." [*Stevenson here falls into the common error of accepting the evaluation of the Macbeths, whose gullibility where witchcraft is concerned is surely one of the strategic points of the play.*] "As we shall see later, the prophecies of the Weird Sisters are in reality a personification of Macbeth's own thoughts; and it would have been possible for Shakespeare to write the play of *Macbeth* without introducing the Weird Sisters at all. But if we were to take out of *Macbeth* the scenes in which the witches appear we should destroy much of the atmosphere upon which the play depends for its effect."

Is that all?

But many editors are less kind than Stevenson to the witch scenes. They are all for omitting the character of Hecate entirely and the scene (III,v) and part of another (IV,i) in which she appears. Moreover, most

theatrical producers follow their example. Sir Tyrone
Guthrie in his *New Stratford Shakespeare,* for example,
doubts that Shakespeare could have written them, and
says of the former:

> "This scene is so incongruous in mannner, so irrele-
> vant in matter, to the rest of the play that I find it
> hard to conceive of its inclusion in any production."

A. C. Bradley, from the literary critic's point of view,
tells us why:

> "These passages have been suspected (1) because
> they contain stage-directions for two songs which
> have been found in Middleton's *Witch;* (2) be-
> cause they can be excised without the least trace of
> their excision; and (3) because they contain lines
> incongruous with the spirit and atmosphere of the
> other witches' scenes . . . they differ . . . in being
> iambic in rhythm."

But Bradley, although he fails to explain his reasons,
believes on balance the passages are genuine and elects
for their retention. Perhaps this is because he realized
the flimsiness of these objections: the first, to anyone
who has ever put a production together, is an idiotic
piece of pedantry; the second is a mere opinion based
on admitted failure to understand the reason for the
scenes' presence; and the third arrogantly assumes that
the "incongruity" was either unintentional on Shakespeare's part or overlooked by his insensitive first editors,
or both. What it adds up to is not an expert opinion
even, but an expression of personal taste. Or perhaps
Bradley's vote for inclusion in the canon stems from
another concern: Bradley comes closer than any commentator I have encountered to grasping an even more

radical implication of the witch scenes in *Macbeth,* and it seems to me possible that he felt uncomfortable at the thought of cutting off further exploration of his own channels of thought.

Our own exploration must begin with Bradley's position that the witches are real people—a thesis argued so brilliantly that one wonders how the myth of their supernaturality or their being "a personification of Macbeth's own thoughts" can still be credited. They are, he writes:

> "not goddesses or fates or, in any way whatever, supernatural beings. They are old women, poor and ragged, skinny and hideous, full of vulgar spite . . . Holinshed (says) 'They were eyther the weird sisters, that is, as ye would say, ye Goddesses of destinee, or else some Nimphes or Feiries.' But what does that matter! unless he used what he read. And he did not use this idea. He used nothing but the phrase 'the weird sisters', which certainly no more suggested to a London audience the Parcae of one mythology or the Norns of another than it does today . . .

> *"There is no sign whatever in the play that Shakespeare meant the actions of Macbeth to be forced on him by an external power, whether of the witches, or of their 'masters', or of Hecate.* It is needless, therefore, to insist that *such a conception would be in contradiction with his whole tragic practice.* The prophecies of the witches are presented simply as dangerous circumstances with which Macbeth has to deal . . . Macbeth is, in the ordinary sense, perfectly free in regard to them . . .

> " That the influence of the first prophecies upon him came as much from himself as from them, is made abundantly clear by the obviously intentional contrast between him and Banquo. Banquo, ambitious

but perfectly honest, is scarcely even startled by them . . . But when Macbeth heard them he was not an innocent man . . . He was tempted only by himself. *He* speaks, indeed, of their 'supernatural soliciting'; but in fact they did *not* solicit. They merely announced events: they hailed him as Thane of Glamis, Thane of Cawdor, and King hereafter. *No connection of these announcements with any action of his was even hinted by them.* For all that appears, the natural death of an old man might have fulfilled the prophecy any day . . .

" 'Still,' it may be said, 'the witches did foreknow Macbeth's future; and what is foreknown is fixed; and how can a man be responsible when his future is fixed?' . . . However it may be with prophecies of actions, prophecies of mere events do not suggest to people at large any sort of difficulty about responsibility . . . The witches nowadays take a room in Bond Street and charge a guinea; and when the victim enters they hail him the possessor of £1,000 a year, or prophesy to him of journeys, wives and children. But though he is struck dumb by their prescience, it does not even cross his mind that he is going to lose his glorious 'freedom'."

In brief, to tell our young students today (as the Stevenson text does) that "in Shakespeare's time the belief in witches was widespread" is to beg the real question. If one asked nowadays "Do you believe in gypsies?" the question itself would be questioned. If it means "Do you believe gypsies exist?" the answer would normally be Yes. But if it means "Do you believe gypsies can perform feats of clairvoyance, phrenology or astrology?" the answer would normally be No—although patently there are thousands of people willing to pay good money to find out.

The attitude toward witchcraft in Shakespeare's day was anything but single, and anything but overwhelmingly credulous. The one contemporary work all experts agree Shakespeare consulted was Reginald Scot's sceptical exposé, *The Discoverie of Witchcraft,* published in 1574, which according to one reviewer of the day "dismasketh sundry egregious impostures, and in certain principal chapters and special passages hitteth the nail on the head."

Scot was pragmatic enough for any modern scientist:

> "But if all the divels in hell were dead, and all the witches in England burnt or hanged: I warrant you we should not fail to have raine, haile and tempests, and now we have: according to the constitution of the elements, and the course of the planets, wherein God hath set a perfect and perpetual order."

Scot pours scorn on the witches' pretensions to magical powers and exposes many of the tricks of their trade: some of them, incidentally, still in use by spiritualist mediums. "But the credit they had," Scot writes, "depended not upon their desart, but upon the credulitie of others." Nor does he spare the attempts of the church hierarchy to play on this credulity when making charges:

> "You must understand, that after they have delicatelie banketted with the divell and the lady of the fairies; and have eaten up a fat oxe, and emptied a but of malmsie, and a binne of bread at some noble mans house, in the dead of the night, nothing is missed of all this in the morning."

It is of course true that Shakespeare's patron, King James, wrote his first demonological treatise as a direct

rebuttal of Scot's *Discoverie,* and ordered all copies of
that impious book burned. In 1604, a year after his arrival in England, he even coerced the parliament into
passing a new and stiffer witch act. But something happened soon afterwards which Shakespeare commen-
tators conveniently fail to mention when adducing evidence to support their conventional view of the witches.

So fluid, so mercurial, was the then attitude towards
the powers of witch-magic that the royal demonologist
changed his mind. In Fuller's *Church History of Britain*
we learn that James, as the result of a series of impostures (mostly by adolescents) gradually lost his faith
in witchcraft:

> "The frequency of forged possessions (by the devil)
> wrought such an alteration upon the judgment of
> King James that . . . he first grew diffident of, and
> then flatly to deny, the workings of witches and
> devils as but falsehoods and delusions."

This change of heart may not have occurred overnight,
but it began with a trial which took place in 1605—the
year after the passage of the witch act, and a year *before
Macbeth* was (according to nearly all modern authorities) written and first performed. In this case the King
contributed £300 towards the exposing of a fourteen-
year-old girl who had feigned hysteria and fraudulently
accused three older women of witchcraft. This would
seem to indicate that James, at the time the play was
written, was already "diffident" about witch claims.

Now slight tremors at throne level, in those days,
customarily produced large waves among those trying
to keep up with the Jameses. It is inconceivable that so
acute an observer of life as Shakespeare, and so know-

ing a student of politics, should have been so *gauche* as to write a play for the King's favour without first ascertaining which way the official wind was blowing. If he wanted to curry favour with James, portraying witches as powerful spirits with a direct pipeline to the Lord of Evil would, at this moment, seem a *faux pas* of the first order. Surely he would more likely suggest in his play what James was apparently beginning to believe: that witches were either sincere but deluded ignoramuses, or outright frauds, or oftener than not (like their modern counterparts) both. Could it be possible he did just that?

This ambivalence would certainly better fit Shakespeare's usually comprehensive and balanced view of life, and better fit his practice in the other plays, wherein while auguries and omens are often used for dramatic effect, a healthy scepticism is always breaking through. "I can call spirits from the vasty deep," boasts Glendower in *Henry IV, Part One:* "But will they come when you do call them?" replies the realist Harry Hotspur. Presumably this raised a laugh from the Elizabethans just as it does from us.

We have no reason, then, to doubt Reginald Scot when he states as a fact of life in his day that "few or none are throughlie persuaded, resolved or satisfied, that witches can indeed accomplish all these impossibilities." But Scot also quotes Seneca to the effect that "the rude people, and our ignorant predecessors *did* believe, that raine and showers"—and presumably other desired effects—"might be procured and staied by witches' charms and inchantments." At the time of *Macbeth's* composition, then, it seems fair to suggest that

witches, like fairies, were universally held to be real
people. King James wrote even in his early *Daemon-
ology*, "they eate and dranke, and did all other actions
like natural men and women." They were known to be
practitioners of the old primitive faith, according to
Scot, to which most of the peasantry and many of the
gentry and nobility still clung, however loosely, and to
which they turned, as we still do, when the local priest
failed to answer life's riddles or the local doctor failed
to cure sciatica. And doubtless, as today, witches succeeded sometimes where priests and doctors failed, thus
prolonging belief in their powers; as Scot said, long ago,
"for it is ods, but they will hit the truth once in a hundred
divinations as well as the best." But about the efficacy of
their charms there was little agreement and much
sophisticated controversy—certainly not universal credulity. For while bright young theologians were debat-
ing whether Satan preferred to possess pretty young
girls or ugly old women, a man so influential as Erasmus
of Rotterdam could write:

> "These witches, through their corrupt phantasie
> abounding with melancholike humors . . . do dream
> and imagine they hurt those things which they
> neither could nor doo hurt; and so they think they
> know an art, which they have neither learned yet
> nor understand."

I find no evidence in all this that an Elizabethan audience, especially one containing King James, would be
scared to death by the appearance onstage of three
witches from the hinterland of Scotland, thunder and
lightning or no.

III

If the views of the audience were divers, what about Shakespeare's own? Let us take a closer look at what he wrote, and the equally instructive things he omitted—presumably on purpose.

First of all, let us note that no one in the entire play refers to the women concerned as "witches," with the exception of the sailor's wife quoted by the First Witch herself: "Aroint thee, witch!" she cries, and it is a deliberate slur. Otherwise the word occurs only in the margin of the text as a direction for cast and stage-management: and the audience was not supplied with programs. In a play denigrating witches one would expect the insult to be hurled often—as it is, for instance by Joan of Arc's accusers in *Henry VI*.

Nor is there any decisive suggestion that they are old. Holinshed, you will remember, called them "Nimphes or Feiries," which might be open to the objection (as an argument) that Shakespeare read but did not use this version of them, were it not for the contemporary (1611) report of a production at the Globe Theatre by the quack, Dr. Simon Forman, which describes the "3 women" as "feiries or Nimphes" and never anything else. Macbeth, it is true, calls them "black and midnight hags"; but then "hag" was used in Shakespeare's day (much as we now use the word "bitch") without necessary connotation of old age. In *Henry VI* the young and beautiful Joan of Arc is called a "hag" by Talbot in the same scene in which he complains she is a "shameless courtesan." Later this demonstrably young woman is called an "ugly witch" and a "fell banning hag."

But you will quote me, I am sure, Banquo's description

of the three witches when he first sees them:

> "... What are these,
> So wither'd and so wild in their attire,
> That look not like th'inhabitants o' the earth,
> And yet are on't? Live you? or are you ought
> That man may question? You seem to understand
>   me,
> By each at once her choppy finger laying
> Upon her skinny lips: you should be women,
> And yet your beards forbid me to interpret
> That you are so."

But the adjective "wither'd" can surely be equally well
taken to apply with "wild" to the attire rather than the
wearer: and "choppy fingers" and "skinny lips" suggest
weather-beaten and starving peasants as easily as they
do age. As for the beards—(you will remember Sir Hugh
Evans in the *Merry Wives:* "By yea and no, I think the
'oman is a witch indeed: I like not when a 'oman has a
great peard.")—is it reasonable to suppose that even
three ancient crones would all be sporting great beards?
Is it not more reasonable to suppose Banquo was seeing
a well-known characteristic of the witches and fairy-
folk, the long straggling uncombed "elf-locks" which
Dr. Murray tells us "are always commented on with
horror by the 'mortal' beholder"? Or perhaps, in addition,
that the three women were wearing primitive masks
over the lower half of the face, as Dr. Gardner tells us
witches did when abroad, to prevent later identification
and punishment? As for their being "black" and "midnight," listen again to Dr. Murray:

> "Eyewitnesses aver that the fairies spun and wove
> their own cloth . . . but their looms were not so very
> satisfactory, and there are many stories extant of

the fairies entering a cottage and weaving cloth on the cottager's loom. The yarn used was generally wool and was occasionally undyed, more often it was green or blue. The colours were dark as in the hunting tartans of the Highlands, and the extremely dark blue gave rise to the belief in the black fairies."

Add to this the dreadful poverty of these early Scottish peasants, and the filth in which scavenging women would have lived, and Banquo's reaction becomes quite logical. Not only that: why should Shakespeare trouble to say in words (in this most economical of plays) what the audience could see for itself? What he is interested in here is not a redundant report on the Witches' appearance but Banquo's attitude towards it: Banquo pours on the ridicule because he is being deliberately abusive.

Bradley has pointed out the contrast between Macbeth's reaction to the Witches and that of Banquo, but not even he has seemed to grasp the plain extent of Banquo's scepticism. We read in Holinshed that Banquo "jested" here; but I have never yet seen the scene played for the ironic comedy that is in it. Banquo states his position quite clearly:

"If you can look into the seeds of time
And say which grain will grow and which will not"—
[which is surely sarcasm!]
"Speak then to me, *who neither beg nor fear
Your favours nor your hate.*"

Banquo—and I do not see how any other meaning can be taken from the words—is telling the women with splendid bluntness that he sees through their flummery and does not believe a word of it.

It is the superstitious and gullible Macbeth who falls for their line. And line it is: for though Bradley says they were not "soliciting" in this third scene of the play, one cannot imagine what else they were doing. Reginald Scot speaks of "the cousening witches, whose practice is above their reach, *their purpose to gaine*, . . . their art uncertaine and full of vanitie." These women lived by their wits. Macbeth was the national hero of the moment; could they have found a likelier sucker? For what else than hope of reward would they stick their necks out? In 1597, in Burton-on-Trent, one Elizabeth Wright agreed to cure a neighbour's sick cow only "upon condition that she might have a penny to bestow upon her god." I submit that Shakespeare's witches were no less practical. They had to be; they were in a dangerous trade and depended upon the goodwill of their clients for their meagre livelihood.

Far from wishing Macbeth harm, in fact, like the black spirits of evil they are usually painted, they plainly wish him well, if only in the way of clairvoyants everywhere: to see their prophecies fulfilled and a new and rich convert made to their occult circle. They have everything to gain by winning his confidence, and everything to lose by frightening, threatening, or alienating him in any way. They are in the same boat as Cranmer when he prophesied for Henry VIII. No: the words and actions of these women toward Macbeth in the opening scenes of the play in no way suggest maleficent spells but rather sincere good wishes. And for reasons which I hope will become increasingly clear, it is of great importance that we avoid attributing to them here motives which Shakespeare explicitly chose not to.

These good wishes they deliver in the form of hopeful and, so far as *they* are concerned, benign prophecies.

The prophecies were easy enough to come by, for women skilled in panhandling, and need no supernatural explanation. As Guthrie points out, there seems no reason why the Witches, as three countrywomen, should not have heard of Macbeth's appointment as Thane of Cawdor:

> "It was uttered publicly by Duncan. It is equally credible that Macbeth and Banquo marching from Fife should *not* have heard the news. The Third Witch adds that he shall be King hereafter, not as a prophecy but as a piece of flattering suggestion and in hope of reward. The remark falls upon ground which is not only fertile but prepared. Macbeth and Lady Macbeth have long pondered the possibility of the crown."

I believe the Witches intend the remark to be *thought* prophetic; as Bradley suggests, the old King Duncan is quite likely to die soon anyway, and the forecast is a simple if adept piece of "conning."

But *Banquo* is not taken in by it! And when he asks mockingly for a similar display of clairvoyance on *his* behalf, the women become much less glib and specific with their predictions. Their prophecies are, in fact, not a whit less equivocal than those little printed messages obtainable today from any penny weight-machine:

> "Lesser than Macbeth, and greater."
> "Not so happy, yet much happier."
> "Thou shalt get kings, though thou be none."

Having just told Macbeth he would someday be king, they could hardly queer the pitch by announcing his successor; the Third Witch shrewdly chooses the next best compliment, and in any case an eventuality which could not be disproved before they all pass on. This is almost the last word they speak before vanishing.

Now why do they vanish so abruptly "into the air"? Surely not because they have frightened Macbeth with Cassandra-like prophecies of doom, but because he has frightened them. They have just handed him the prettiest compliments imaginable, and his friend Banquo too for good measure but, far from getting a penny or two for their pains, they are brutally hectored and placed under plain threat of physical attack. They wisely clear out fast.

And vanishing neatly into thin air was no more complicated a trick for witches than for our own North American Indians, especially if the scene was, as Forman reported, "a wod," and not the "desert place" of the editors' imagination. Dr. Murray writes:

> "The fairies had a disconcerting habit of appearing and disappearing when least expected, a habit which seemed magical to the slow-moving [villagers]. Yet dexterity in taking cover was only natural in a people who must often have owed their lives to quickness of movement and ability to remain motionless."

But sometimes witches merely went home and literally dropped out of sight; their houses, says Dr. Murray,

> "were circular in plan, and were sunk in the earth to a depth of two or three feet . . . The hearth, when there was one, was in the middle of the one chamber, and there was an opening in the roof to allow the smoke to escape. Such houses . . . when overgrown with grass, bracken and small shrubs, would appear like mounds or small hills."

Remains of these mound-huts have been found recently in Britain, so their authenticity is beyond question. Could they, I wonder, have been the "bubbles" in the earth referred to by the logical Banquo? And would that not have been the meaning taken from his little joke by the Elizabethan audience?

And did they really "hover through the filthy air"? Not a bit of it: Shakespeare only has them say they can, which is quite different. Says Dr. Gardner flatly:

> "No witch ever flew through the air on a broomstick or anything else, at least not until aeroplanes came in. There is indeed a fertility charm to bring good crops which is performed by riding on a pole, or broom, as a hobby horse. Doubtless ancient witches practiced this rite, leaping high to make the crops grow."

And we know that they did take drugs which give a sensation of flying, just as they do to the modern "hipster," so they may easily have believed they flew, which is no reason for us to credit impossibilities.

We do not see the Witches again until the famous scene in Act III, when they meet their superior, Hecate. But before we do so too, there are three details in the earlier scenes which claim attention.

It has always bothered sensitive poetic souls among the commentators—and which of them is not?—that the Witches descend at the drop of a pointed hat into base doggerel, much more to be expected from hacks like Middleton than from the divine Shakespeare. But if we credit Shakespeare with knowing what he was doing we must assume he had a reason. And there is one: it is now established that witches did in fact speak in doggerel, not only when casting spells, but when together on religious occasions, much as the modern Cockney uses rhyming slang on somewhat dissimilar occasions. They believed that rhymes would bind powers they sought to assume. To our generation, so poetically inarticulate, it may seem odd that illiterate countryfolk should show skill at this, but we have Scot's word for it that "they can rime either man or beast to death." And Shakespeare had plenty of models aside from Middleton. Here is a sample of an Elizabethan translation of Virgil:

> "Inchantment plucke out of the skie,
>   The moone, though she be plaste on hie:
> Dame Circe with hir charmes so fine,
> Ulysses mates did turn to swine:
> The snake with charmes is burst in twaine,
> In Medowes, where she dooth remaine."

I think Shakespeare's Witches improve on Virgil. And he is most careful to have them speak in prosier style when the talk is not religious, although many editors since his time have laboriously rephrased such lines into regular verse, destroying this useful difference:

> "FIRST WITCH: A sailor's wife had chestnuts in
>   her lap,
>   And mounch'd, and mounch'd,
>   and mounch'd:
>   Give me, quoth I.
>   Aroint thee, witch, the rump-fed
>   ronyon cries.
>   Her husband's to Aleppo gone,
>   Master o' the Tiger:

Then listen to the spell begin as she drops into rhyme:

But in a seive I'll thither sail,
And like a rat without a tail
I'll do, I'll do, and I'll do."

Then what about those "obscene dances" and that
"capering" mentioned by Dover Wilson, if not by Shakespeare? Once again we have what was to the witches a
religious rite mocked by prejudice. Dr. Latham says:

"The dance was not an individual capering but a
ceremonial round . . . They left their fairy rings
('whereof the ewe not bites': *Tempest*, V,i) on
nearly every heath of England."

This is not to read things into the text which are not
there; it is the "obscene capering" which is not there.
Shakespeare's knowledge of the rites, if we are to judge
by such evidence as existing signs of these ancient
"rings," and still existing practices reported by Gardner
and others, was full and accurate. Writes Dr. Latham:

"Of all the Elizabethans who made mention of them
(the fairies), there is no one who showed himself
more cognizant of the belief in their existence, and
no one who featured more prominently their traditional power and activities."

His "thrice to thine, and thrice to mine, and thrice again
to make up nine" is more than a bit of hocus-pocus; it
fits the choreography which Dr. Gardner describes as
traditional among modern celebrants. And his later list
of items for the witches' brew is, so far as we can tell,
equally authentic. Dr. Gardner gives a long list in his
book, *Witchcraft Today*, of such ingredients and their
uses in country districts in modern times. The items may
sound a bit unsavory to us, but it helps to remember that

many of the names refer not to the real thing but to exotically-labelled herbs.

One of the most telling uses Shakespeare makes of his knowledge of witchcraft lies in a detail so small it has, so far as I am aware, been entirely overlooked. That first short witches' scene ends with the introduction of a cat called Graymalkin, the First Witch's familiar. Now the *domestic* familiar—as we know from court records as early as 1587—was used *only for working magic, never for divining.* And yet what these three women are setting out to do—to prophesy—involved not magic but divination. The cat, that seemingly insignificant detail— and I do not wish to magnify it; it is a clever "plant" only—is a dead giveaway that these witches are in beyond their magical depth; they ought not to have been divining at all. The historical fact is that among witch groups "divination was the peculiar right of the priesthood" (*Encyclopedia Britannica*):

> "As the power was always incomprehensible, not to say freakish, it was necessary that it should be approached by those who knew the right methods."

And Shakespeare tells us by more than the dragging in of a cat that the art of these witches was limited. The First Witch tells us plainly enough herself, in a speech that is usually cut or gobbled out in jig tempo, that her brand of magic goes only so far. "Though his bark cannot be lost," she says of the sailor she is hexing, "Yet it shall be tempest-tost." Now unless it could not be lost by virtue of her own limitations as a witch, one cannot imagine why; other, more powerful witches sank ships with alarming frequency, as King James and the whole of Britain had good cause to know. What these witches *can* do, as they tell us in the plainest possible language, is to raise a wind or hex a sailor, both feats of simple magic, utterly unrelated to the divination they are about to practise. Could Shakespeare have put the contrast between their reach and their overreach any more forthrightly in dramatic terms?

Might it be, therefore—if you will go along with me for the sake of argument—that three green, and possibly young—I do not insist upon it—witches, just such "cousening witches" as Reginald Scot referred to, "whose practice is above their reach, their purpose to gaine, . . . their art uncertaine and full of vanitie," set out to earn an honest (or dishonest) penny by performing a rite they do not understand? They say the proper litany and do the appropriate little dance: "the charm's wound up." Confronted with the object of the charm, Macbeth, and by unhappy chance, his sceptical colleague, Banquo, they show a little nervousness, natural enough in sorcerer's apprentices. Why else do they caution silence by laying their fingers on their lips, and need to be coaxed into saying the piece they had prepared? After their forthright encomiums to Macbeth, however, their set-piece is said, and instead of thanking and rewarding them, Macbeth "starts" and seems, according to Banquo, "to fear things that do sound so fair." This is disconcerting enough; but when Banquo mockingly asks for his own horoscope, they realize they are in deeper water than bargained for, hedge lamely, and disappear in sophomore terror when Macbeth threatens them. Their well-intentioned and harmless trick has gone wrong; the apprentice witches have nearly blown up the lab.

And when we meet them next, naturally enough, they are getting hell for it from the boss.

IV

And that brings us to the celebrated Hecate scene, which nearly all editors and producers find expendable, which they believe can be excised, as Bradley says, "without the least trace" of its excision. Hecate, as a few of the editions will tell you, is The Queen of the Night, but none that I have encountered tell you that both names were honorary titles afforded the high-priestess of the local group of witches.

The first thing we notice here is that the three lesser witches pretend innocence: "Why, how now, Hecate! you look angerly." But playing innocent does not help them, for Hecate has apparently been brought up-to-date on their caper from another source. That source as we have learned from the previous scene, is Macbeth himself, for there he tells Lady Macbeth that he has a rendezvous with the Weird Sisters on the morrow. Now unless he planned to return to the scene of their first encounter and simply walk around until he bumped into them, he would have no means of finding them—except, perhaps, from the local priestess, whose identity would be known to most people. (There is some evidence priestesses wore a sort of uniform.) From Hecate, then, we learn that he has indeed made an assignation through her to meet the sisters on the morrow at the Cave of Acheron, a locale probably suggested by Hecate in view of a cave's eminent suitability for all the paraphernalia of a seance, including a dim light, trapped smoke, and a built-in echo. Hecate herself is apparently not supposed to be there, for she later hustles backstage when Macbeth arrives; but she goes to great lengths to organize it personally.

And then Hecate spells out for us in the most unmistakeable terms, in case we missed the point in the earlier scenes, the impudence of her charges in invading her right of divination:

> "Have I not reason, beldams as you are,
>   Saucy and overbold? How did you dare
> To trade and traffic with Macbeth
> In riddles and affairs of death;
> And I, the mistress of your charms,
> The close contriver of all harms,
> Was never called to bear my part
> Or show the glory of our art?"

Does this still seem "irrelevant" to the earlier scenes? And then she states equally plainly—in case we missed it before, and anyway it is time we were reminded—that she knows their intentions were good if misdirected:

> "And, which is worse, all you have done
>   Hath been but for a wayward son,
> Spiteful and wrathful; who, as others do,
> Loves for his own ends, not for you."

Could the "others" be the Christians?—the witches commonly referred to Christians as "the others" and apparently regarded them as self-seeking materialists, much as Buddhists think of Western Christianity today. In any case, the point she makes is that their attempt to perform white magic has had the blackest effect, since **Macbeth has murdered twice as a result of it.** Along with the rest of Scotland, she plainly considers Macbeth

a bad specimen. But unlike most of her fellow-country-
men, she determines to do something about it, using
the only means at her disposal. (Gardner tells us the
witches of England hexed Hitler during the last war.)
She immediately says to the others:

> "But make amends now: get you gone,
> And at the pit of Acheron
> Meet me i' the morning: thither he
> Will come to know his destiny:
> Your vessels and your spells provide,
> Your charms and every thing beside.
> I am for the air; this night I'll spend
> Unto a dismal and a *fatal* end."

Now this seems to me a highly courageous woman; she
proposes to kill the tyrant single-handed, while the rest
of Scotland is still arguing the pros and cons. Where is
your "foul hag" and "creature of ill-omen" now?—on
the side of the angels! I do not see how anyone can avoid
seeing that the witches, at this point in the play, are, in
the simplest dramatic terms, aligned with the good guys
against the bad guy.

Bradley comes very close to seeing all this:

> "When Macbeth sees the witches again, after the
> murders of Duncan and Banquo, we observe . . . a
> striking change. They no longer need to go and
> meet him; he seeks them out. He has committed
> himself to his course of evil. Now, accordingly, they
> *do* 'solicit.' They prophesy, but they also give ad-
> vice: they bid him be bloody, bold, and resolute.
> We have no hope that he will reject their advice;
> but so far are they from having, even now, any
> power to compel him to accept it, that they make
> careful preparations to deceive him."

But Bradley apparently failed to notice that these careful preparations are referred to only in the very scene he says can be excised without a trace!

Nor do the witches, of course, *want* their advice to be taken; they merely want to "draw him on to his conclusion," as Hecate says, by making him feel secure: "And you all know, security is mortals' chiefest enemy." The preparations she makes for this are indeed elaborate. She knows that Macbeth, prompted by the fulfilment of the earlier prophecies (brought about not by the witches but by him, to their horror), is credulous in the extreme, and she is confident he can be imposed on by smart conjuring. So, after telling the women to bring their "vessels," "spells" and "charms," she sets the scene for the seance.

> "Upon the corner of the moon
> There hangs a vaporous drop profound;
> I'll catch it ere it come to ground;
> And that distill'd by magic sleights
> Shall raise such artificial sprites
> As by the strength of their illusion
> Shall draw him on to his confusion."

Magic sleights-of-hand, *artificial* spirits, illusions—did you ever hear a fraudulent frame-up more clearly indicated? If Shakespeare intended his witches to *have* supernatural powers, or to be the personification of Macbeth's own thoughts, taking us backstage to see the stage-management cooking up the special effects would seem a curious way of convincing us.

The witches, of course, exactly like many modern mediums, believed in their own hocus-pocus even while contriving it. The broth they are making when Hecate arrives at the Cave of Acheron, and on which she con-

gratulates them, is for them a genuine charm. And when
Hecate tells them that "everyone shall share i' the gains,"
she must, I suggest, mean more than the dubious satisfaction of performing an evil deed, for that is precisely
what they do not think they are doing; by their lights
they are doing right: by engineering Macbeth's downfall they are "making amends" for their earlier lapse.
When Macbeth abruptly enters, incidentally forcing
Hecate to retire to the shadows from which she presumably masterminds the special effects, he asks them
point-blank what they are doing. They could scarcely
tell him, and answer with admirable diplomacy, "A deed
without a name." But at this point he is the only one
who does not know its name: ritual murder by witchcraft.

The ceremony is a solemn one, given added horror not
by supernatural intervention but by the very fact that
we know Macbeth is being taken in by a fraud. That
the text intends this is shown by what follows: a whole
compendium of legerdemain, familiar to anyone privy
to spiritualist stunts, from disembodied voices, echo
effects (the thrice-repeated name business), ghostly
apparitions and accompanying thunder-noises off, to—
so help us!—a distorting mirror:

> "And yet the eighth appears, who bears a glass
>   Which shows me many more."

Shakespeare could have found it all, and doubtless did,
in Reginald Scot, in the chapter entitled "Of divers
wonderfull experiments, and of strange conclusions in
glasses, of the art of perspective, etc." Even that Mac-

beth is able to see the ghost of Banquo at the end should not surprise us, when Scot says:

> "For you may have glasses so made, as what image or favour soever you print in your imagination, you shall thinke you see the same therein."

We have a fine explanation even for the "sinking cauldron" in a note of Dr. Murray about the witches of Alsace: "The cauldron was overturned . . . The spilling was to bring about fog, the rising steam being the sympathetic magic to bring it about." I can think of no more sensible act on the part of the witches to cover their retreat inside the cave and to drive Macbeth from it.

Let us note finally that nowhere in the play does anyone but Macbeth blame the witches for malfeasance of any sort, and that despite their known prophecy of his kingship, known to Banquo and later to Lennox, at least, no move to charge them or punish them in any way is ever suggested. A reasonable explanation might seem to be that they did, indeed, "make amends."

Now I cannot help thinking that the maligned little episode at the end of Act III is the linch-pin to this whole sequence of events, that its contents jibe with and re-inforce the earlier scenes (when understood without prejudice), and that the witch scenes supply far more than a mere atmospheric background; taken together they supply an absolutely essential factor in the structure of the play. If my view is right—and I have tried not to distort the play to fit a preconceived theory but rather to elucidate the text as it exists with the light of our increasing kowledge of witchrcaft—if I am right, then the tragedy of Macbeth seems to me not less but infinitely greater. For then the action develops from a ghastly mistake: the road to hell for Macbeth is paved with the good intentions of the Witches.

Almost as if he felt impelled to compensate in some degree for presenting such sympathetic heathens, in his fourth act Shakespeare goes to some pains to get in a scene at the English court where a deliberate comparison is made with Christian ways. The effort is not unaccompanied by dramaturgical dislocation; you will remember that a conversation between Macduff and Malcolm is summarily interrupted. Here we learn how the saintly King of England employs the approved Christian arts of healing by laying-on of hands, the touch of holy objects, and prayer to the authorized God. Moreover, his "gift of prophecy," in comparison with the witches' pagan fumbling, is, says Malcolm, "heavenly." This scene, so essential to the religious balance of the play, is also usually cut in performance.

I have had no time to pursue the ramifications of these ideas through the rest of the play, whereon they have a great bearing, or to discuss certain obscure passages on which they throw some light. But I hope I have said enough to stimulate you to look at the play afresh yourselves.

Bradley, of all the commentators, comes closest when he says:

"*Macbeth* leaves on most readers a profound impression of the misery of a guilty conscience and the retribution of crime . . . But what Shakespeare perhaps felt even more deeply, when he wrote this play, was the *incalculability* of evil—that in meddling with it human beings do they know not what."

And witches were, and still are, human beings. Macbeth is surely a greater tragic hero if the crime is not the witches', but his. As Reginald Scot wrote in 1584, and Shakespeare unquestionably read before 1606:

> "Let us also learn and confess with the prophet David, that we ourselves are the cause of our afflictions; and not exclaim upon witches, when we should call upon God for mercie."

NOTE:

One of the questions asked after the lecture concerned the Witches' "Fair is foul and foul is fair." It seems to me that this jingle is open to a variety of interpretations, (for example: "We'll turn this foul day into fair weather for us!"),—except the one perhaps most freqently given it: "Evil is our good." This might be the expression of a Christian theologian's opinion of witchcraft, but would hardly be uttered by witches, who believed themselves to be every bit as pious and "good" as the Christians. Such an interpretation is open to another objection: it spoils the dramatic irony. If the irony is to work, it must be Macbeth's later "switch" on the line which has the sting, not the prior statement. I believe the Witches are only repeating a witch jingle meaning little more than "It's an ill wind which blows nobody good"; the ironic joke is then completed later when Macbeth, with his "So foul and fair a day I have not seen," etc., inverts the meaning. It is he, not the witches, who turns their predictions ("things which do sound so fair") into an excuse for evil-doing. It is therefore he, not they, who makes foul of fair.

Herbert Howarth, a member of the Seminar staff in 1960 also, was Scholar of Christ Church College, Oxford, from 1935 to 1939. Among the posts he has held was that of Director of the National Book League in London from 1950 to 1954: he is now a member of the Department of English at the University of Manitoba. He is the author of *The Irish Writers*, published in 1958, and of *Figures behind T. S. Eliot,* to be published in 1962.

HERBERT HOWARTH

An old man looking at life

HENRY VIII AND THE LATE PLAYS

Was Shakespeare an "old man" when he wrote *Henry VIII*? One or two scholars at this Seminar smiled when I first said so—scholars who happen to be 47 or 48 and are at their hard-hitting best. But everybody who comments on the late plays subscribes to one myth or another, and I like the myth that the Elizabethans and Jacobeans did everything earlier than we do: took degrees earlier, married earlier, campaigned earlier, rotted earlier. Shakespeare had led a busy existence, and it may be fair to call him an old man at 48.

On the evidence of *Henry VIII* and the preceding "romances," what were Shakespeare's interests and theatrical objectives in the years when he felt himself to be the veteran; when sometimes he despised the newcomers to the theatre and thought himself a Lafeu among Bertrams; when sometimes he felt outstripped and saw himself as the Antony among the boy Caesars; when sometimes he felt a master-artist, a Glendower become a Prospero?

It had been his habit, in the days when he was occupied full-time in the theatre, to set himself with every new play a fresh problem: to make it a matter of pride,

as Eliot, working from his example, has made it, not to
repeat himself. He might write two plays about a husband consumed by jealousy, but in one he would imagine
an unsophisticated man victimised by an adroit enemy
and entirely deprived of help, while in the second he
would deliberately reverse the conditions and show a
man surrounded by friends and good advisers but pol-
luting himself in defiance of them, victim of "the imposition . . . Hereditary ours." In *Henry VIII* Shakespeare
seems in some respects to have broken his self-imposed
rule. Perhaps he decided, when the Players (needing
a special work for the marriage of Princess Elizabeth)
pressed him for a script under his pension agreement,
that he would comply with the least possible exertion.
He rapidly drew a play together around a theme he had
used before: the evolution of a paternal monarch.

For that is the spine of his last play. At the outset
Henry is well-meaning, innately good, but easily fooled.
These cardinals trifle with him, so do the aristocratic
intriguers. He is duped into the condemnation of Buckingham. He is decoyed into abandoning a good wife.
He drops his Cardinal, half decoyed into it, half finding
his own way. At last he learns sovereignty. He who was
duped into destroying Buckingham is not duped into
sacrificing Cranmer. He dominates the intriguers, is
master in his own house. He is lonely, but with the
loneliness of a king or God, the watcher, the penetrator
of motives, the ruler.

But how much more elaborately he had graphed the
evolution of a king, the father of the country evolving
out of a boy ashamed of his father, in the three plays
about Hal. Then he was elated by the theme; the whole

conception was a discovery; he presented it in brilliant detail. In 1612, resorting to a similar interpretation of Henry for no better reason than to spare himself labour, he presented it concisely.

It is one thing for a writer to decide to throw a work off carelessly, another thing to do it. His interest stirs despite himself. If the emergence of the king never quite heated Shakespeare, which is perhaps why it has often been invisible to critics, some of the material associated with it did. For example, the description of court-intrigue. Here again he was on ground he had covered before. The "convention," as we say, the convention that a poet's business is to denounce the vices of the Court went at least as far back as Skelton, in whose days *Henry VIII* is set. Shakespeare had often used it (and at least once, satisfying his appetite for change, had deliberately refused it and imagined Leontes' virtuous retinue). Why is there vitality in his last version of it? When he retired from London life, the experiences of the capital took new shape in his memory. His business in the past had sometimes carried him to the fringes of the court, and he had seen that there was a good deal of truth in the literary legend that courtiers, the best and the worst alike, live destructively on each other's blood. Now he ruminated on the matter with an old man's pleasure in understanding human behaviour. Consider how he enjoys his control of the diplomatic material in the play. Of the same order, and more pervasive, is his enjoyment in the delineation of intrigue. With taut skill he shows how ambitious and envious men combine against the favourite of the hour, down him, split, and re-combine against the next favourite: faction begetting faction, injury begetting injury, as crime begat crime in the early plays of the Roses.

His object in the first scene was to establish the tone of intrigue. But it was not very festive material and might chill the nuptials. He preluded it with a vivacious flourish, the story of the Field of the Cloth of Gold; and with his practised capacity for making everything co-operate in his total design, he connected this with the theme of grandiose ambition. But in his initial plan, before he had recognized all his themes, the intrigue was his concern, and he meant to lead with it in the first scene and to establish Norfolk as the type of the aristocratic court-schemer. The director at Stratford brought out Norfolk's role clearly; Leo Ciceri's agreeable features were transformed, built up and coloured to suggest malignancy, whispering in corridors, proscription in locked rooms.

Shakespeare had at first chafed at the commission to write *Henry VIII*, thought it a burden to be discharged as rapidly as possible. Then as the drafting proceeded, he warmed up to the pleasure of anatomizing intrigue. Then, the warmth spreading, other questions opened up —not fresh topics, but questions that had long taxed him and his contemporaries. Above all, the problem that was to underlie *Paradise Lost* half a century later: the human constitution and why evil is compounded with the good in it.

The ancient riddle of the human constitution had descended to Shakespeare in a peculiar, provocative form. The English dramatists of 1600 were children of the Humanists; they would not have been doing their work but for a hundred years of Humanism. The Human-

ists had presented them with a dilemma: on the one
hand, the conception of man as capable of everything,
endowed with a creative faculty of godlike stretch, on
the other hand, an aversion for the animal in man. The
academics had simply condemned carnality, as in man
but not of man, as "ab-hominable," to be ignored or
censured or mortified. "The worst part of the human
picture," said Ascham, "is from the navell downwards."
Shakespeare was familiar with this view. Sometimes he
lent it to his characters. Sometimes they uttered it in
torment:

> But to the girdle do the gods inherit,
> Beneath is all the fiend's.

The dramatists could not ignore sub-navel man. They
insisted on studying him, bringing him near and en-
larging him. Therefore that predominant impression
of blood, violence, lust, which the plays of the great
English epoch convey. And if they often echo denuncia-
tions borrowed from the Humanists, denunciation is not
really their tendency. Their tendency is to reconcile the
upper and the lower man.

For man doesn't really dislike his lower half. Not even
a Humanist. Not even Holofernes. The daughters of the
parish profit very greatly under him. Construing Shakespeare's dialogue as Shakespeare intended, Michael
Langham, in this year's matchless *Love's Labour's Lost*,
had Holofernes tweak Jacquenetta; and his actor
tweaked to perfection, switching away with a look that
both denied that he'd done it and watched for the result,
Kate Reid's beaming simper of comprehension and con-
sent.

Shakespeare undertook an intricate consideration of Holofernes' problem in *Measure for Measure*, analyzing a Deputy, whose name shows that he claims, like the Humanists, to be in action and apprehension an angel, but who falls prey to his abominable weakness. The outcome is a justification of the lower self and the Fall: "best men are moulded out of faults," if only mercy be granted. This is Shakespeare's version of Milton's "justification," and it is the better version, though it is true that Milton had disadvantages (he was not free-minded, not flexible; he was too ambitious, seized with the conception of a mighty work; he was so enamoured of philosophy that he forgot men, and when he remembered men he didn't understand them) and true that, like every artist, he made a miracle of his disadvantages. But it was not Shakespeare's final verdict in the case. Neither in *Measure for Measure* nor any other play was Shakespeare attempting a final verdict (Milton was—that was his crushing disadvantage). Shakespeare was the artist who undertakes an adventure with an idea, undertakes Durrell's act of play, adopts a point of view, "tries it on," enables us to experience the possibilities of it without hazard. Then he has a go at the problem again with a different hypothesis.

In *The Tempest* Shakespeare invented an amusing new approach to the Humanists' problem. He imagined a girl who has been brought up seeing no one but her father (who's a half-god) and a monster (who's a half-devil). Suddenly confronted with man, what will she think? First she sees the Prince. Of course, that's an easy one:

> I might call him
> A thing divine, for nothing natural
> I ever saw so noble . . .

Later comes the real test: she is shown a collection of court-intriguers and scoundrels, with the decent old Gonzalo *solus* among them to indicate the proportion of good to bad in any human sample. Now what has she to say? She still likes them:

> How many goodly creatures are there here!
> How beauteous mankind is!

Prospero drily comments

> 'Tis new to thee.

Her welcome, with its love of life and its reminder that that means love of man, including bad men; his aged scepticism, and the compassion for the illusion of youth that underlies it: this concatenation, this comedy, brightens the debate, and the brightness is a vote for life. But the old Shakespeare was multiple-sighted, not content to leave us or himself enjoying that pleasant flight of fancy. He simultaneously tried a different adventure with Caliban: there *is* an element of lust and devilry which is beyond society and beyond cure:

> on whose nature
> Nurture can never stick; on whom my pains,
> Humanely taken, all, all lost, quite lost.

In Caliban he rejected the beastliness of man. Not the rascality of man: Stephano and Trinculo, who have no sense of beauty and who have suffered nothing, he tolerated, as nothing worse than clowns and inebriates, and licensed them to recognize and scorn the beastliness or fishiness of Caliban, as if even a fool, even a knave, knows the difference of beastliness and detests it. To modern taste this is not very agreeable, and we struggle against it and claim that Shakespeare half-awares discerned the heroism of the suffering beast: some rights Caliban has and they have been violated, some instinct for beauty has been moved in him but it is thwarted. But perhaps we should try to be as tough as Shakespeare in trying the feel of dramatized hypotheses. Caliban is one of his hypotheses.

The matter was still vexing him when he wrote *Henry VIII*. It is implicit in the recurring use of the word "angel." The Spanish queen, whose isolation among enemies Shakespeare presents so compassionately, reproaches the English.

Ye have angels' faces, but heaven knows your hearts.

Shakespeare is alluding to the story, which Camden had included in his *Remains*, and which has become part of the national mythology, of St. Gregory's serious joke: a joke itself at once humanitarian and Humanist, at once in love with human beauty and sad at human shortcomings. Let us ignore the momentary flash of national self-criticism in the allusion; it is "ahead of its time," as we can see in the contrast with Iago's joke about English drunkards, which is a piece of self-indulgence. The point for us is that the line echoes the "angel" images of *Hamlet* and *Measure for Measure* and implies the whole long debate whether man be angel or beast. There are at least two other "angel" passages linked with it. The Lord Chancellor, baiting Cranmer, says we are not angels,

> We are all men,
> In our own natures frail, and capable
> Of our flesh . . .

Wolsey compares himself with the most spectacular of
the angels, Lucifer, and warns Cromwell, warns the
audience, against the sin of ambition, which must lead
to downfall.

Henry VIII is a play of tragic falls: the fall of Buckingham, following his father's pattern; the fall of a good
Queen; the fall of a Cardinal not good but grand. Critics
have said that the play is essentially *De Casibus*. Indeed,
it is. But it is not merely a catalogue of falls in the old
style, nor does it merely rely on the explanation of
"Fortune's wheel" (that consolation to those who fell,
that delusive hope of those who were oppressed and
never rose, that *memento mori* and incentive to charity
in those who fared well; and that excuse which put
events beyond human power and so tended to make
men shallower, less self-critical, less reforming). Instead
it defines the human context of political crashes; it
attributes them to men and explores the process; makes
men self-critical. And it adumbrates a theological justification of these falls and the Fall. What justification?
That the tragic *casus* induces what otherwise we would
never come to: knowledge of ourselves. Here Shakespeare's persistent attempt to vindicate human weak-
nesses intersects with another interest of his which had
been developing for some years.

The two rules from the temple at Delphi, the rules
which Socrates professed, "Nothing in excess" and
"Know thyself," were touchstones of the sixteenth-
century writers. Certainly they were Shakespeare's

touchstones. Perhaps his contemporaries detected their importance in his art; there may be that rare thing in English Renaissance compliments, a genuine sense of parallel, in the second term of the eulogy under the bust in Trinity Church at Stratford-upon-Avon:

> Judicio Pylium, genio Socratem, arte Maronem,
> Terra tegit, populus maerit, Olympus habet.

The middle compliment was deserved. Shakespeare with his inquisitive and analytical intellect was the most Socratic of English writers.

It is a commonplace of drama that the characters gain in knowledge as a play evolves. That does not make every dramatist a Socrates. Roxane grows from love of a pretty face to love of a mind, but Rostand is not a Socrates. Shakespeare is not a Socrates in the early plays, for though his characters acquire knowledge and even self-knowledge he does not yet know it. Richard the Second grows in consciousness from the hour of surrender at Flint Castle through the scene of deposition to the last days in Pomfret Prison; but Shakespeare nowhere calls the process, and the extremity of pain that accompanies the last verbal gymnastics, the development of "self-knowledge." I'm not sure where he begins to talk about self-knowledge. As far as I've noticed, it is in *Measure for Measure:*

> Of what disposition was the Duke?

asks the Duke from the cover of his hood, and Escalus assures him

> One that above all other strifes contended especially to know himself.

knowledge and self-knowledge come to Lear: he has
been blind to the state of his kingdom and its iniquities,
and of his family and its inner oppositions, but when he
breaks on his pride he learns to know them and to know
himself. In the late plays the action rewards the characters with self-knowledge. Those lines which captivat-
ingly sum up *The Tempest* tell how

>   In one voyage
> Did Claribel her husband find at Tunis,
> And Ferdinand, her brother, found a wife
> Where he himself was lost, Prospero his dukedom
> In a poor isle, and all of us ourselves
> When no man was his own.

In *Henry VIII* the idea is strung across the play. When
the nobles are intriguing against Wolsey, Norfolk says
"The king will know him one day," and Suffolk answers
"Pray God he do! he'll never know himself else." It's
not clear whether Suffolk means "Otherwise Wolsey will
never see himself as he is, but will continue to act the
god" or "Otherwise Henry will never escape from Wolsey's shadow and see himself as the King with his duties
and powers." Both results follow from the intrigue.
Wolsey falls and:

> *Cromwell:* How does your grace?
> *Wolsey:*   Why, well!
>   Never so truly happy, my good
>   Cromwell.
>   I know myself now.

And **Griffith**, making his charitable apology for Wolsey,
arrives at the same point of repose

> His overthrow heap'd happiness upon him;
>   For then, and not till then, he felt himself . . .

Of course, Wolsey's end is more than repose; it is virtue. In his new tranquillity Wolsey plays the good master: he sends Cromwell to Henry's service and shelter; and this is the sign of virtue, for fidelity in master-servant relations, especially if the master falls, is another Shakespearean touchstone (inherited this time not from Delphi but from the Anglo-Saxons). His end is virtue and triumph. It is the justification of Lucifer's fall. Best men are moulded out of faults, alike the faults of their bodies and the more dangerous faults of the head—the faults of the Humanists themselves. They will climb insolently, fall terribly, and come to perfection in the fall.

To translate is to go further than Shakespeare would. But certainly his mind plied these matters as he wrote *Henry VIII*, his interest fully awakened.

What about his interest in the verse?

A decade after Shakespeare's death, Ben Jonson complained that audiences expected the dramatist to gratify the eye. In the theatre of the fifteen-nineties to which his first contributions had been made, the ear had been paramount, that ear wise with centuries of music, sermons, story-telling. To set the boys gaping there had been such appurtenances as the "creaking chair" let down on cords, but these were crude and inconsiderable. The trouble began when machines and properties underwent a sudden improvement, when Inigo Jones brought engineering and the visual and three-dimensional arts to Court, when Jonson and Jones collaborated, and Jonson saw with disgust that Jones took the honours— lavish fees and all the attention. The brilliant spectacles of the Court the public theatres quickly aped (and started the trend that has turned the theatre from a thrifty to an extravagant and risky financial enterprise). The King's Players were evidently ready enough to go with the stream. From 1607 or 1608 Shakespeare manipulated his scripts to provide opportunities for the engineers and pleasures addressed to the eye. *Pericles* has its storm and its theophany, and its adventures in costume, *Cymbeline* its theophany, *The Winter's Tale* its storm, its sheep-shearing revels, the unveiling of the statue, *The Tempest* a wreck, a magic banquet which appears and disappears, and a masque that is half a theophany. Evidently when *Henry VIII* was contemplated, the company decided that it must be particularly sumptuous, an appeal to the eye more compelling than anything the general public had experienced so far. In performance it was "set forth," as Sir Henry Wotton's letter describes, "with many extraordinary circumstances of pomp and majesty, even to the matting of the stage." Together with processions and pageants, Shakespeare provided, in accordance with his recipe of the period, the half-masque, half-theophany of Katharine's vision.

Henry VIII was a play to delight the eye. But did Shakespeare think, as Ben Jonson thought, or pretend to think, in 1625, that when the eye was indulged the ear lost its pleasure? He saw no reason why. The innovations rather stimulated his verse. It was in the very epoch of engineering and costume that he conducted his dramatic poetry to fresh enterprises.

I will suggest half-a-dozen of his experiments in half-a-dozen telegraphic sentences. He tried his hand at a strongly sculpted poetry for the classical pomp of the

theophany in *Cymbeline*. He took further than ever before—and he had already gone far with it—a style based
on the broken and repetitive phrases of intense speech;
we hear an amazing elaboration of it at the end of *Cymbeline* (Iachimo is making his confession, and the
broken phrases register the suffering of a wounded man
as well as shame), and we hear it in Henry's rebuke to
his Council for misusing "this good man." He developed
the terse style in which he makes his impact with a series
of nouns:

> ... holy oil, Edward Confessor's crown,
> The rod, and bird of peace ...

or:

> A narrow lane, an old man, and two boys ...

or:

> ... did you not name a tempest,
> A birth, and death?

and this is a style which has helped to form the taste of
the present day since Eliot's percipience rediscovered it
and Eliot's skill brought it back into use. Concurrently
he took pleasure in bursts of sensuous, almost oriental
metaphor, as in that line, "The fringed curtains of thine
eye advance," which Coleridge loved. This is the obverse of the naked style, just as the obverse of the speaking style is in that dignified inversion with which Henry
advises Cranmer

> The best persuasions to the contrary
> Fail not to use, and with what vehemency
> The occasion shall instruct you ...

There Shakespeare looks forward to Milton. Elsewhere
he works for a style of clear pointmaking which looks
forward to the epigram and clarity of those poets of the

next hundred years who, taking the opposite path to
Milton's aimed at making English as civil a language
as French:

> He gave his honours to the world again,
> His better part to heaven, and slept in peace.

The couplets of *Othello* and *Coriolanus* had tended in
the same direction. It is not too much to say that all the
styles of later English literature can be educed from
Shakespeare's middle and late plays.

But especially from the late plays. You will find there,
for example, what you will scarcely find in the middle
plays: the Arcadian rhetoric. "But that is found in the
early plays! It brims over in *Richard III*!" Yes, so it does.
It *is* used in *Richard III* and swamps some of the scenes.
Shakespeare thought for a spell (in defiance of the good
sense of *Love's Labour's Lost*) that a tragedian must
delight his audience with the Arcadian artifices. But
they led the play from drama towards opera, and he
realized that his theatre stood in need of greater naturalism, and dropped them and worked towards poetry
completely wedded to character and action, which he
established with a first splendid mastery in the *Henry IV*
sequence. But, absent from the middle plays, the Arcadian rhetoric is deliberately and delightedly employed
in the late. And now Shakespeare does what had been
beyond his range in the early nineties: uses the figures
Sidney and Spenser loved and uses them without modu-
lating into opera; uses them without digressing from
character; integrates them in the poetry of action. So
the lines about Camillo who tardied the command

> ... though I with death and with

Reward did threaten and encourage him,
Not doing't and being done . . .

and the lines about the shepherd's old, hospitable wife

. . . her face o'fire
With labour and the thing she took to quench it.

The non-naturalistic figures are now fused with Shakespeare's naturalism. They do not hold up the drama; they hasten it; make the language not only more energetic but more concise.

All these experiments Shakespeare felt he could the more safely venture when his theatre was gratifying the eye more abundantly.

And he felt free to interpose more frequently scenes in which the characters gather not to act events but to report them. He had, of course, exhibited his pleasure in the poetry of narration some time before the era of the pageants: he had written Hotspur's speech about the fop on the battlefield, Casca's speech about the offer of the crown to Caesar. I leave it open whether "The barge she sat in" and Octavius' hardly less brilliant passage about the retreat from Modena preceded the pageant-period or belonged to it. But Shakespeare used his "reporting" poetry more in the late plays than before, and a great deal in the last of his plays. In *Henry VIII* he included the narratives of the Field of the Cloth of Gold, of Buckingham's trial, of Anne's Coronation, of Wolsey's death. To look at the placing of the last two passages is to see how beautifully Shakespeare developed an art of exchange between the eye and the ear. The voices fall silent and the Coronation procession crosses the stage, magnificent to the eye. Then the voice takes over, the gentleman describing the scene in the Abbey. Immediately follows the scene at Kimbolton, the voice of Griffith narrating Wolsey's last journey. That is immediately followed by the theophany, the masque of the spirits of peace. So the appeal flows from one sense to the other. More than that: Shakespeare incorporates with the new technique his old trick of significant juxtaposition. The new Queen's glory displays the old Queen's poverty, her triumph in Westminster Abbey displays the melancholy of Wolsey's passing in Leicester Abbey, the celestial vision revealed to Katharine displays the impermanence of Anne's triumph. The older he grew, Shakespeare, like all the masters, grew the fonder of "form," the more susceptible to the pleasure of proving that he could fetter himself and still move freely, as he does in this last play.

Proposal of toast

When we speak of Shakespeare, there are at least three aspects of a personality involved. First, there is a man who lived like other men and died three and a half centuries ago. About this man we know very little, and even less that is really significant. We know that Ben Jonson loved him, and Ben Jonson did not love easily— he described his wife, as I remember, as "a shrew yet honest." But we have no authentic likeness of Shakespeare, for I certainly do not regard the goggle-eyed mask that stares vacantly at us from the frontispiece of the Folio as an authentic likeness of any human being, much less Shakespeare. Second, there is the dramatic poet whose plays are acted in this unlikely spot, simply because it is called Stratford, and have brought thousands of people from all over the continent to flutter around his genius like moths around a light. When we look at the variety of people who come to see and hear these plays, we realize that the first remark ever made about Shakespeare's admirers is still the best one. It is the opening sentence of the preface to the Folio: "From the most able to him that can but spell: there you are numbered."

But there is a third and a still greater Shakespeare. We can express ourselves only within the limits of a language that has been made articulate for us by our great writers. We can think only within the limits of ideas and concepts that have been worked out by our great writers. We can understand one another only within the limits of the social vision of our great writers. And there is, of course, no greater writer than Shakespeare. So, whenever we open our mouths to speak, the rhythms and cadences of Shakespeare are helping to form what we say. Whenever we think, or think we think, Shakespeare's metaphors and images are entering into the structure of our thought. Whenever we attain any understanding or love of one another beyond the range of our immediate experience, Shakespeare's insight into humanity is helping to make our insight possible.

It is an act of sentiment, perhaps even of sentimentality, to honour the memory of a poet who has been dead for centuries. It is only ordinary courtesy to honour a poet who has entertained us as royally as Shakespeare has done this week and on so many other occasions. But to honour the poet who has played so large a part in forming our own mental processes is an act of piety. It is like pausing a moment to be grateful to the air we breathe and the water we drink.

Will you rise and drink with me a toast in memory of the Shakespeare who was for an age, and in honour of the Shakespeare who is for all time.

Dr. A. W. Trueman has been Director of the Canada Council for the Encouragement of the Arts, Humanities, and Social Sciences since 1957. Before that he had held a diversity of appointments including that of Government Film Commissioner and Chairman of the National Film Board as well as the Presidency of the Universities of Manitoba and New Brunswick; the earlier part of his career was taken up with the teaching of English at Mount Allison University. He is a graduate of Mount Allison and Oxford.

A. W. TRUEMAN

Shakespeare,

A PERSONAL VIEW

Perhaps I should begin honestly by saying that I have only a vague notion of what my assignment is this evening. When I sat down to think about my speech, I had been carrying with me, for a month or two, a general impression that I had been asked to reply to a toast to Shakespeare, not too seriously, and in an entirely personal way, that I had been excused from any attempt at scholarship—and that is just as well—and that this attractive exercise was to be accompanied, at least for my listeners, by coffee, port, cigars . . . About then I discovered that I had fallen into a cunning trap. The imagined circumstances of this address were so charming—an atmosphere of easy good fellowship, almost of unbuttoned leisure, a kindly disposition on everyone's part to laugh readily at even the most modest witticism —that they obscured two harsh facts that in the end could not be set aside: the audience would know a great deal about Shakespeare, and the speaker would know very little. On re-reading the correspondence with Professor Jackson I discovered that he had written "the audience will be listening to experts *of one kind or another* during the rest of the week, and we feel that the personal touch"—it was kind of him to avoid saying 'the inexpert touch'—"may be best suited to this occasion." The invitation to be personal is, of course, delightful to me. Any man—and the women will bear me out—loves to talk about himself, and the material is inexhaustible! At any rate you are going to hear, for the next few minutes, the unabashed use of what someone has called the "perpendicular pronoun." But it seemed to me, and it still seems to me, that it will be difficult to bridge the gulf between us, even by amiable intentions on both sides and the help of a relaxed, tolerant, well-fed, after-dinner mood. To comfort me in this dilemma, and to suggest that not all the advantage is on the side of you scholars, I turn to these words from *Love's Labour's Lost*:

> "Small have continual plodders ever won,
> Save base authority from others' books.
> These earthly godfathers of heaven's lights,
> That give a name to every fixed star,
> Have no more profit of their shining nights,
> Than those that walk and wot not what they are."

What I shall have to do, then, is dredge up from memory anything about my own experience of Shakespeare that may be of at least mild interest to others, and may in some measure reveal the problems that confront *you*, the experts, as in one way or another you seek to mediate between Shakespeare and the average man.

Last year you listened to Mr. Robertson Davies at this hour, speaking, I gather, under terms of reference exactly parallel to mine. But *Mr. Davies* and I are in no

sense parallels. He is an author, a critic, a scholar—and
he gives his life to being these three. I, alas, am a rene-
gade professor, an administrator—generally thought to
be the lowest form of life by a group like this—and at
best, a reasonably cheerful distributor of other people's
money. My qualifications for making this speech have
been steadily shrinking for the last twenty years. It is
therefore without mock modesty that I suggest you
regard me this evening as a representative average man,
as far as the theatre is concerned.

My first acquaintance of Shakespeare must have been
that of countless others. It came through the one-
volume, family edition, not a scholarly edition, but the
ponderous, expensively bound, rather ugly production
designed to meet the needs of all who had been persuaded that no household should be without the works
of the *Bard*. And for the frontispiece there was the
Droeshout engraving. I wonder how many thousands
of young people have turned from Shakespeare in dis-
may when they first caught sight of this forbidding
picture? The high forehead moving back into singularly
unattractive baldness of pate, the staring eyes expressive
of nothing, the heavy jowl and the sensuous lips: all
this displayed, as it were, on a platter—the starched ruff
which separates the head completely from the body.
If Droeshout had deliberately set himself the task of
creating the face of a man who couldn't possibly have
written the works of Shakespeare, he could scarcely have
been more successful. Could this man actually have put
down these words in the familiar sonnet, perhaps over-
familiar, but nevertheless worth reading again—and
again:

"Shall I compare thee to a summer's day?
  Thou art more lovely and more temperate:
  Rough winds do shake the darling buds of May,
  And summer's lease hath all too short a date:
  Sometime too hot the eye of heaven shines
  And often is his gold complexion dimm'd,
  And every fair from fair sometime declines,
  By chance or nature's changing course untrimm'd.
  But thy eternal summer shall not fade,
  Nor lose possession of that fair thou ow'st;
  Nor shall Death brag thou wanders't in his shade,
  When in eternal lines to time thou grow'st:
  So long as men can breathe, or eyes can see,
  So long lives this, and this gives life to thee."

No, there is no "intimation of immortality" in those dull eyes, no reflection of the sensitivity and the imagination and the passion that could pour out all this loveliness for another human being, no matter who that being may have been. He couldn't possibly have imagined a young man saying a heart-broken good-bye to a beautiful woman—wanton though she was, but not to his knowledge—in these words:

"Injurious time now with a robber's haste
  Crams his rich thievery up, he knows not how;
  As many farewells as be stars in heaven,
  With distinct breath and consigned kisses to them,
  He fumbles up into a loose adieu,
  And scants us with a single famished kiss,
  Distasted with the salt of broken tears."

The Droeshout Shakespeare simply couldn't have done it!

Without being more than half serious about all this, I must say that I think the Droeshout engraving has been a misfortune. It is too bad that there has been the continued association of this forbidding, unpromising drawing and Shakespeare. How much better it would have been had we never found it, and been forced to adopt as the symbol of Shakespeare the handsome portrait of some unknown Elizabethan gentleman who looked as if he might have some poetry in his liver.

Well, the ugly one-volume edition, and the Droeshout engraving combined to create the atmosphere of Sunday afternoon gloom that surrounded Shakespeare for so many young people of my generation in the Maritime Provinces of Canada. And what the schools did to us helped very little to dispel the gloom. I was taught one play in high school, *Julius Caesar.* It was presented to us as a narrative based on historical events, and dotted with memorable speeches. We were required to have such detailed knowledge of the play that we could give the meaning of every word used in any way differently from the custom of our time, spot any quotation that might be presented to us—that is to say, attribute it to the speaker, place it in the right act and scene and explain in elaborate detail what it meant—write plausible character sketches of everyone in the play. I do not recall that at any time it was suggested that this piece of literature was designed for production on a stage in a theatre; nothing of it was ever acted out either for us or by us; we were not asked even to imagine what all this might be like if seen on the boards in front of us. All the exits and entrances and all the indicated action of the piece were mere words. We had never seen a Shakespearean play, and the assumption, apparently, was that we never should. In fact most of us had never seen a play of any kind. Occasionally in the town of Truro,

Nova Scotia, where I lived, some Church group or some social society would attempt a play, usually involving foreclosed mortgages or the abrupt and convenient re-appearance of long lost heirs, but nothing calculated to arouse curiosity about the theatre, or likely to reveal in any degree the peculiar excitements and other rewards of playgoing.

It is a wonder, then, that any interest in Shakespeare survived among my contemporaries in that area of Canada. I suggest that such an interest did not in fact survive, unless here and there, in an individual to whom *poetry* insisted on making its appeal, triumphant over the inadequate presentation of the dramatist. As a matter of fact I was fortunate in one teacher who took me in hand when I was about sixteen years of age. Without being a fine scholar, he was scholarly; he was sensitive to the subtle use of language, and he made me work. In my own home there was a literary feeling which compensated for the indifferent collection of books on our shelves. My father, who was a professor of animal husbandry at the agricultural college in Nova Scotia, could quote Keats, if not endlessly, at least for minutes at a time. I learned early, therefore, something about the magic of words used with new and strange connotations, in lines that moved in rhythms my teachers, alas, seemed not to notice. Pieces that I read then, indifferent pieces, many of them, survive in my mind now because of some chance appeal made to the feelings by a combination of words that had for me something of this new and mysterious magic of poetry. "The Burial of Sir John Moore" which I was put through, or—if you prefer—was put through me, survives for nine words only, "the ran-

dom gun that the foe was sullenly firing." They still
evoke mystery for me.

Well, what I am trying to do here is give you a little
glimpse of a society in which there was no theatre, and
no possibility of a theatre; where Shakespeare was a
literary artificer of long ago who put fine speeches into
the mouths of imagined or historical men and women,
strung these together on a thread of narrative that
wouldn't bear too much weight, and frequently employed a kind of linguistic form that we were told was
blank verse and probably poetry, whose language was
usually quaint, and often incomprehensible, whose
characters were conspicuously unlike the citizens of
Truro, and lent themselves to amateur psychoanalysis.
In short, he was a highly examinable subject, by virtue
of his difficult language, his unusual characters and his
improbable stories; so much so that even a modest
degree of ingenuity on the part of the examiner was
quite enough for the satisfactory humiliation of the
reluctant student.

Out of this I moved into college where I was under
the tuition of a fine scholar who had a dry mind and a
horror of emotion. The amateur theatricals of the college, in my time, never rose above the level of such a
play as *The Romantic Age*, by A. A. Milne, in which
I played, with some embarrassment and even shame,
the part of a young lover who—if my memory is correct—
was caught off balance, so to speak, in the cavalier costume he had worn to a ball. The ingenious producer of
this play, no doubt with higher things in mind, had me
sing unaccompanied, to the advancing figure of my
intended sweetheart "Oh Mistress Mine, Where Are

You Roaming?" to the music of Roger Quilter. This, until I got to Oxford was my nearest approach to Shakespeare the playwright.

At Oxford—and it was largely my own fault—this history pretty well repeated itself. I simply was not theatre-minded. Perhaps I was encouraged in my disposition to regard Shakespeare as a book to be read, and nothing more, by Neville Coghill's first vacation assignment: "Trueman, what are you planning to do with yourself over the Christmas holidays? Oh? Well, read all of Shakespeare before you come back." Once again I went at it, reading the plays, soaking up the poetry, jotting down learned—I thought—annotations and critical profundities in margin and notebook. (I still have a few of the texts I used in those days; to look at the pencilled comments on their pages is now almost too painful an experience.) Because no one as yet had really put the issue to me, and because I had been brought up in an almost playless society, my curiosity didn't direct me to the theatre. As I have said, I soaked up the poetry of the plays, and I haunted the concert halls to listen to Bach, Beethoven, Mozart, Schubert, Chopin, and Brahms, as presented to my astonished and ravished Maritime ears by Schnabel, Paderewski, de Pachman, the Lener Quartet, Casals, Thibault, Cortot, and a host of others.

I saw but two Shakespearean performances during my Oxford days—with shame I admit it—and *they* were of the same play. The one was presented in Oxford by the O.U.D.S., with Peter Fleming playing *Iago*, and Val Dyal playing *Othello*. The other was at the old Savoy Theatre in town, with Paul Robeson in the name rôle.

No doubt he confirmed my bias of interest in the poetry, for I recall over the passing of 32 years how he declaimed the great purple patches, apparently at me, in a voice deep, resonant, passionate, and incredibly moving.

Back in Canada I taught Shakespeare to a second-year class at Mount Allison University, and I taught it as you would expect: with decent reference to the scholarly work that had been done on the texts, and to the Elizabethan world in which they had been born and produced, and with a low bow to A. C. Bradley, but with no reference, or almost none, to the plays as *plays*, designed for the theatre and successful for that purpose as no other body of plays by one author has ever been; and I probably spent at least half of each lecture period in reading aloud the passages I loved. That this was an inadequate presentation of Shakespeare I do not deny, but that it kept the name of Shakespeare alive in a few minds and helped these to a love of his poetry I think I have evidence to claim.

Then when I was nearly 50 years of age, came Stratford, Ontario, and with it the beginning of an annual bout of Shakespeare playgoing. I should imagine that my sense of wholly new adventure was shared by thousands of Canadians, although no doubt the inhabitants of Ontario had had greater opportunities to know something of the theatre, in early life, than we had had in the Maritimes. You will see now that I meant what I said when I asked you to think of me as representing the average man, at least as far as the theatre is concerned.

It is impossible for me to say what this experience of Stratford has meant, to explain what it has revealed about the plays themselves and about the theatre. By what magic, I have asked myself, are these "books" given this exciting physical being? How brought to life in front of me—active, brawling, teeming, shouting, violent, quiet, tender, humorous? These and more epithets come flooding in as I cast my mind back over the performances of the last few years.

But, trained as I had been, or perhaps I should say, *not* trained as I had been, I miss sometimes, even in this paradise of Shakespearean "buffs," the poetry. Let me explain what I mean. I don't mean what was meant by a critic who in connection with one of last season's productions spanked the director for not having realized and brought out what he called the "poetic element" of the play. I am puzzled by this usage. It seems to me that poetry is *words:* words selected and put together as only genuine poets are able to do. A so-called "poetic scene"—in Nature, I mean, not on the stage—can only be a scene that may stimulate a poet to write poetry. What other meaning can be accepted? But this phrase is an absurdity, because any scene may do that, or at least be one of the elements in the complex of stimuli that move a poet to the exercise of his art. If we mean that a scene is romantic, or tenderly pastoral, has grandeur or mid-summer magic about it, we should do better to say so. And by the same reasoning, the "poetic element" in a play must be, according to my thinking, nothing other than the poetry of the play: that is to say, the words in it that have been chosen and put together in the ways that we commonly recognize as making poetry.

When, therefore, I say that I sometimes, even here in Stratford, miss the poetry, I mean simply this: that the players do not always give the lines that are true poetry in such a fashion as to bring out the fact of their poetic form and nature, and create in me the peculiar and deep satisfaction that the hearing of poetry, properly spoken, gives me. This, and nothing else, ought to be called the "poetic element" of the play. How much better to call it simply the "poetry" of the play.

Now at this point it will be obvious to you that your speaker is in no sense a critic of the theatre. As a matter of fact, I don't approach a theatrical performance in a consciously critical frame of mind. When I go to the theatre, I have, thank God! no need to write anything about the play later that night for the papers next morning. I have put down my five dollars for the best seat I can get, and usually another five for my wife, and I have undertaken the tiresome journey from Ottawa for the purpose of being entertained, of living once again within the magic of the theatre, of enjoying an exhilarated sense of community with the other members of the audience, the rapport between those of us in the seats and the players on the stage, the something that I can hint at only in this feeble way, whatever it may be that is the particular virtue of the theatre to give to those who love it. And I am prepared to go more than half way to meet, receive, and be in sympathy with the players, and to adopt an attitude to my fellow human beings there beside me that transcends, believe me, the customary work-a-day disposition of Ottawa. And I am prepared to believe that the playwright, particularly this playwright, the director and the players know much more about this play, plays in general, and the theatre than I do.

I don't ask, therefore, for very much. But one thing I do ask for. And that is that the divine poetry of the greatest poet who ever lived shall be delivered to me, out of the plays in which he enshrined it, *as poetry*. I know all the plays that are presented here. I refresh my memory of them before I come. And I wait, I confess, and it may be wrong of me to do this—but I wait in this scene or that scene, for the words, used as only Shakespeare has ever used words, that have echoed in my mind and heart for years. And I don't want any theory of realism, naturalism, or dramatic propriety to get between me and my poetry! It seems to me wrong and false to Shakespeare that a player should be so occupied in "acting," so busy with "business" deemed appropriate to the occasion, that the delivery of immortal poetry is put in the third place. For example, poetry rapidly delivered as excited prose ceases to be poetry. Having aired this personal prejudice I am quite prepared to admit that Mr. Langham, or even some lesser director of Shakespeare, could no doubt show me in five minutes how hopelessly wrong I am. But this is the way I feel about it. I'm being personal. On invitation. More of the same!

I don't mind a bit if the player, when he has to deliver a considerable speech, an "aria"—to use Michael Langham's words—rich in poetry, steps out ever so little from the framework of the play and the event that is taking place, and addressing himself to me, and using all the resources of a talent that has been trained for the purpose, gives me, unmistakeably, the poetry. Recently in Vancouver, I heard Isaac Stern play a concert and at the same time conduct an excellent chamber

orchestra. When the adagio movement of the Haydn
Concerto in C Major came along, the other first violins,
the seconds, the violas, the oboe, and the other instru-
ments involved, retreated subtly into the background,
Mr. Stern stepped forward about a foot and a half, and
addressing himself to me, accomplished the ravishment
of my mind and heart that was my hope in coming.
No analogy, particularly in the arts, is ever perfect, but
I suspect that there is a parallel here that has some
validity. And wrong-headed as many of you may think
me, I suggest that in my underprivileged condition perhaps I represent one of the problems that directors and
producers have to face.

Now as I draw to the end of these unscholarly, highly-
prejudiced, and unashamedly personal remarks, may I
say that nothing I have said should be taken as a major
criticism of, or disagreement with, the direction of our
theatre here in Stratford. I for one am very proud of
this theatre. It may well be the finest Shakespearean
theatre in the world. I find myself resenting the annual
strictures of my old friend and student, Mr. Nathan
Cohen, who, I have sometimes thought, may by now
have pushed himself into the position, described by
F. L. Lucas, where his "greatest pleasure consists in
being displeased." I seek only to make the point that
Shakespeare, though he is a great craftsman of the stage,
a profound analyst of the human heart, and one of the
great humorists of all time, is also—in my book—the
greatest poet who ever lived, and that this shining fact
ought never to be lost sight of in a theatre that bears his
name. It has seemed to me that now and then, even
here, other concerns and responsibilities are allowed to

cloud this truth. This is perhaps not a bad time to say these things, since the plays we are offered this season, taken as a group, are not so rich in poetry as many of the others, and no one will therefore construe my little essay as a piece of immediate criticism. No doubt I have been guilty of over-emphasis; and by this time you may wish to quote *Love's Labour's Lost* against me as I, good-naturedly, quoted it against you, by suggesting that I begin to remind you of

> "One, who the music of his own vain tongue
> Doth ravish like enchanting harmony."

Last year, Mr. Davies came to an end by remarking that he had not forgotten that he was replying to a toast to Shakespeare's memory, and he said "I am certain that he would wish me to thank you very much." I echo Mr. Davies' opinion, and in this wonderful, New-World home of Shakespeare, where it may be assumed that all honor is consistently done to him as the great conqueror of the stage, I venture, most humbly, to thank you on behalf of the ghost of Shakespeare, the poet.

POSTSCRIPT. It is only honest to admit that on the evening after this speech was made, I attended the Stratford performance of *Love's Labour's Lost* in which the poetry of the play was never lost sight of, and the delivery of the passages I waited for was beautiful beyond my power to criticize.

B. W. JACKSON

Toast to Shakespeare

Mr. Toastmaster Smith, Mr. Crow, ladies and gentlemen:
It must, I suppose, have occurred to most of us that
this occasion, this gathering tonight, belongs to one man
alone, and he born almost four hundred years ago. Because of that and because we suspect he was a genial
man who loved good company, it is fitting that we do
honour to his memory here tonight with some jovial
ceremony. In this, I suspect we serve an ancient tradition. There must have been a first occasion long years
past when in a London tavern, perhaps on such a summer's night as this, a little group of noisy players, happy
and excited by their afternoon's success in a new play by
a new playwright, drank to his health as he sat among
them. And since then on how many occasions has his
name been honoured, how often explicitly in words and
wine, how more often implicitly in the thoughts and
actions of men both alone and in company? Surely no
man has given so much to so many: in countless times
and innumerable places, in a babble of tongues to a multitude of saints and sinners until we come across time
and an ocean to this place of festival, to this Ontario
town named after his birthplace, to this theatre and to

us, we happy few who meet to honour him here. Among this company of scholars and entertainers who know him and who love him well, in humility and with enormous pleasure as spokesman on your behalf, I would like, then, to propose a toast to the greatest of entertainers—an epithet I confess I hold in honour and in awe—to the greatest of Englishmen to the poet and playwright: WILLIAM SHAKESPEARE.

J. W. Crow, lecturer in English at King's College, London, was educated at Charterhouse and Worcester College, Oxford. From 1928 to 1940 he was a journalist and sports reporter in the English provinces, London, and New York, later teaching at Wellington College. Since joining the Department of English at King's College he has visited North America on several occasions and has been a visiting professor at the University of California at Los Angeles and at Northwestern University; in addition he has worked at the Institute for Advanced Study of Princeton University, and the Folger, Huntington, and Newberry Libraries. His edition of *Romeo and Juliet* will be published in the New Arden Shakespeare; he contributed the article on Shakespeare in the *Encyclopaedia Britannica*.

J. W. CROW

Call for
the Robin Redbreast

Why have I been chosen to speak on behalf of William
Shakespeare? I say to myself, "Do I resemble William
Shakespeare?" I say to myself, "Do I resemble any particular character of William Shakespeare's?" I remember that two years ago I was staying in the Shakespeare
Hotel in Stratford, Warwickshire, which named its
rooms after the characters in the plays. When I arrived
there I found that I—all 280 pounds of me—had been
allotted a room named "Peaseblossom." That irritated
me slightly; I thought that their method of choice was
to a certain extent offensive until I discovered that my
dear friend, my dear, kind, good, delightful, sweet, Miss
K. M. Lea of Oxford, was in "Quince."

I have been wondering almost up to the very last
moment what should be the title of my address and I
have been thinking of a number of titles which I have
heard at various times. I heard one once by Professor
Wilson Knight which was entitled "My Methods and
What They Have Taught Me." I thought that wouldn't
do, but I thought that I might perhaps call it "My Pig-
headed Rushes and Where They Have Landed Me."
But even that I was against, and I thought of the lines

by William Blake,

> A robin redbreast in a cage
> Sets all heaven in a rage

and I thought of those people who, in connection with Shakespeare, set me in a rage; my robin redbreasts. My title is in fact borrowed from *The White Devil* by John Webster and is: "Call for the Robin Redbreast." Who are the heretics who stray from my own brand of orthodoxy, the people who drive me to distraction and put me in a rage? (Need I add that I really do know that it was the cagers and not the caged who maddened Blake?)

When I arrived in this country at Malton airport on Sunday last, I had, not being an American or a Canadian, to undergo the full rigors of the immigration people. I wasn't stripped to the bone, beaten with a rubber truncheon and finger-printed; though you have to imagine the kind of scene, which I would like to put in comic strip form, between me and the immigration man. The immigration man said, and you must imagine the balloon coming out of his mouth, "What is the purpose of your visit?" So I said, with a balloon coming out of my mouth, "I've come to see some Shakespeare plays." So he said, "I'll put down purpose of visit—pleasure." I didn't reply, but I thought (with, no doubt, a balloon coming out of the back of my head), "Boy, are you out of touch with modern trends of criticism!"

My subject then is those I am opposed to. You are particularly requested not to shout a lot of abusive comments to me when I become intolerable, because this whole business is being recorded. The last time this happened to me was when I delivered a speech in Madi-

son, Wisconsin, and they had a tape-recorder secreted
about the place, and I have been since then, I gather,
five times pirated by a certain American radio station;
so at five-minute intervals I intend to say, aiming my
remarks particularly at this little machine, "Copyright
by J. Crow, 1961."

The first heretic I should like to pillory is the person
who is opposed to the theory that Shakespeare's plays
are for pleasure. I'm with the man at Malton airport on
that, body and soul. The people on the other side of
the fence, who are, I think it is (alas) fair to say, university professors and school teachers and similar brain-
washers, do seem so very often to hold the view that
Shakespeare used to get into his little room, stroke his
little beard, and say, "Now I must sit down and write 45
more lines of material for a Ph.D. dissertation." That
would seem to me a bad view. I do not think he wrote
his plays for that purpose. I do not think he wrote his
plays in order to have something to bury a lot of philosophy in. Nor do I think that he wrote plays so that they
might be concealed propaganda pamphlets in favour of
the Earl of Essex or in favour of Tudor theories of law
and order; nor to persuade people to accept the succession of James. I think he wrote plays for the fellow members of his company to take part in and act, and to
attract customers to the box office.

I think that we are not often enough told that Shakespeare was not only a dramatist who wrote for the
theatre, but also a dramatist who wrote for a given
theatre and a given theatrical company. When he was
writing something for Hamlet to say, he was also writing
something for Richard Burbage to say, as Hamlet. If he

were with us today he would be writing something apt for Mr. Campbell to deliver as Henry VIII. He would not be writing something merely for *an* actor, but would be composing with given actors in his eye for a very large number of parts in his plays. This seems to me a thing that is true and is worth bearing in mind.

One often reads the nineteenth-century learned books, which tell you various delightful things about Shakespeare's changing ideals of womanhood. It may, it seems to me, have been less a change of ideal than the fact that the person for whom he had written his last few leading female roles had unfortunately suffered from a breaking of the voice, and a new person of the Rosalind-Viola-Girl-Guide type had now become the leading "actress" in the theatre.

Among my enemies, my robin redbreasts, are the wild theorists. If you want to be opposed to me as a heretic, do so, but may you be besought to follow a certain number of laws in this matter? I often read a book and discover that Chapter One ends with the words "it may then be tentatively suggested that . . . ," whatever it is. I turn over the page and the opening words of Chapter Two are "As I have proven." One comes across this too often. If you are going to be a wild theorist, you ought to do your homework and know what the state of the market is, and not make statements that are absolutely against popular belief. It's no good simply saying,"as two plus two equals five, it therefore follows that . . . "; you have to prove the case.

I here, according to my notes, enunciate for the first time before any audience what is known as CROW'S LAW. CROW'S LAW seems to me a very valuable one, and those who are taking notes would do well to do it in red. CROW'S LAW is: "Do not think what you want to think, until you know what you ought to know." Get your background right before you start getting to these matters.

Something else comes into this business of persuading other people to one's own opinion. When I have succeeded in persuading myself of something, it's just too boring for me to have to recapitulate it all to persuade other people later. So I try to slip it in, in a kind of crookedy manner, saying, "The consensus of scholarly opinion is," or something to that effect. In this way, one doesn't have to do the tedious work of proving something; one simply puts it in some such snobbish way and then says, "The best people believe this, and I'm not going to take the trouble to prove it."

A major clutch of robin redbreasts can be found on this side of the Atlantic more than in England. If one goes to a dinner party, a kind, good, well-educated, well-spoken, and civil man speaks to you and says, "Teach English, do you?"

I say, "Yes, at an English university."

Then he says, "What do you teach?"

And I reply, "I teach Shakespeare."

"Shakespeare; yes, who do you think wrote it?"

And I say, "I think Shakespeare wrote it."

"Well, I don't think the case for Lord This or Baron That or the Marquis of the Other has ever been properly refuted, do you?"

The last time this happened to me the man had the kindness to say, "Does this bore you?" He had the surprise of his life when I answered.

There is this curious feeling that these plays are so good, and they make a string vibrate inside so many people, that they couldn't possibly have been written by an ordinary person. Could this be the work of a countryman, uneducated, middle-class, provincial? No. It must be a courtier, a peer of the realm, a university graduate. This seems to me to be a particularly idiotic and unintelligible form of lunacy. If you're going to have a miracle, and I think the plays of Shakespeare are miracles, it doesn't seem to me any more likely that you're going to have this miraculous egg laid by a peer of the realm than by the product of Stratford-on-Avon Grammar School.

What I do find strange about this matter, is why one has to suffer it. I don't know how it happens to you people, you Shakespeare experts, but I, as a Shakespeare expert, when I go to a dinner party, do not drive a general into a corner and give him my views on strategy. I do not take an eminent medical man and tell him my theory about that as yet undiscovered vein which goes from the pancreas to the ear, and say that doctors ought to try curing diabetes by massaging the lobes. Why do they victimize Shakespeare experts in this way? They don't do it to people in other trades as far as I can make out. Let us have no more of these people.

Let us have no more of these people who judge a Shakespeare play as though it were an attempt to be the shortest distance between two points. A poetic play is not a straight movement from point A to point B. It isn't a straight motor freeway, it's a rambling country road. Take an example from *Henry VIII*. There is a direct way of saying "we won't tell anyone." The way the man says it in the play is "This may be left to some ears unrecounted," which I think better. If anyone rebukes Shakespeare for doing that kind of thing, you have my full permission to call him a redbreast of the first order.

I am worried by the various efforts that are made by people to draw attention to the irrelevancies in a play, and to draw deductions from these irrelevancies. In an exceptionally admirable edition of *Richard II*, Professor Matthew Black went out of his way to speak quite sharply to Shakespeare for losing control of himself and wasting time on all that irrelevant junk about Queen Mab in *Romeo and Juliet*. Shakespeare is so much in love with words, says Professor Black, that he holds up the action of the play in this particular scene.

I personally think that the irrelevant in a Shakespeare play is very often the pleasurable. (I hope that the irrelevant is often the pleasurable for other people, otherwise you'll start throwing things at me, because I don't stick to the point very much.) It doesn't seem to me that the Queen Mab speech *is* irrelevant. The play of *Romeo and Juliet* is concerned with various goings-on between a couple of people, and this couple of people is, to a very large extent, shown to us by the surrounding characters. Romeo is a person who is put into a framework, he is not just slapped down stark naked on the stage. He is what one might describe, among other things, as a member of the Mercutio gang. The depicting to us of what kind of a person Mercutio is, is an important thing in showing us what kind of a person Romeo himself is. If one doesn't have the Queen Mab speech, one gets a Mercutio who is a witty, dirty-talking young man; but this speech adds, on top of that, another feature, and it makes a poet of him. There is also "the atmosphere" in a play, and it is very often the irrelevancies that are exceptionally operative in the gathering together of atmosphere in a play. It's a thing that one finds in a Shakespeare play; you find it still more in the plays of John Webster.

When you read a Shakespeare play, you're engaged in doing two things. You are thinking about the play; but you are, even though people tell you not to, also thinking about the hen that laid this particular egg that is giving you so much pleasure. I think you can learn a great deal about Shakespeare from the irrelevancies. When there are strayings from the source material; when you get someone who is enormously filled out in the Shakespeare play, as compared with what he was in the source from which Shakespeare drew it—as is Mercutio, as is Enobarbus in *Antony and Cleopatra*, as is the Bastard in *King John*. These are things which Shakespeare wasn't bound to put in; they weren't in his source. They were things he put in, as far as I can guess, for his own pleasure. I think they are the things that can be used adequately and virtuously for thinking about this problem of "what sort of a man was Shakespeare himself? How did his mind work?"

In the play of *Antony and Cleopatra*, Mark Antony lost the battle of Actium because North's Plutarch told Shakespeare so. But Enobarbus was the kind of man that Shakespeare made him: the cynical soldier who was also the poetic man and the mouthpiece for that superlative passage beginning "The barge she sat in, like a burnished throne." I think that Shakespeare is there using Enobarbus as a poet. Enobarbus does not say this

the fall of greatness is stressed in the play.

Buckingham saying in Act 2, scene 1,

> The last hour
> Of my long weary life is come upon me.
> Farewell!
> And when you would say something that is sad,
> Speak how I fell.

Act 3, scene 1, Katharine saying,

> . . . for I feel
> The last fit of my greatness . . .

Next scene, Wolsey saying,

> Farewell
> The hopes of Court! My hopes in Heaven do dwell.

Wolsey earlier in the same scene saying,

> Nay then, farewell!
> I have touched the highest point of all my greatness,
> And from that full meridian of my glory,
> I haste now to my setting. I shall fall
> Like a bright exhalation in the evening,
> And no man see me more.

and then,

> Farewell! A long farewell, to all my greatness!

I should say that it is a curious thing that several times in this play one does get this business of the fall of greatness shoved in front of the eye. I should go on to point out that this fall of greatness happens to excite Shakespeare to the writing of, I think, the best verse in the play.

I don't like people who say that the main theme of a Shakespeare play is this one thing, or that one thing, or the other one thing. But an important theme in most of the history plays is the study of the inadequate king; and very often, if it isn't the inadequate king, it is the inadequate great man, the man in position. I should go on to say this is very largely linked up with the medieval idea of tragedy, as you get it expounded in Chaucer; tragedy being concerned with people who are in high estate, and then come down to low estate, and finish in misery. It is the keynote of all these things for which the Elizabethans had a strong enthusiasm; and this enthusiasm is exceptionally difficult for people in the twentieth century to share.

I should say this business of the fall from greatness brings into Shakespeare's mind the fall of those whom we could almost describe as the stock great-fallers, the angels who from pride fell from heaven; and he compares them with meteors and bright exhalations. Another line which I feel fits in with this theme comes in *Macbeth* when Malcolm says,

Angels are bright still, though the brightest fell.

I think the people who drive me most mad are those stage directors who are determined to go one better than Shakespeare; who can always assist by giving their own genius to help the poor old crippled bard. You remember the beginning stages of *Richard II* where there is a good deal of argument, almost coming to blows at times, between Mowbray and Bolingbroke. Bolingbroke throws a number of charges at Mowbray, and anyone who cares to read the history books knows that the charges made by Bolingbroke were justified, and that Mowbray was guilty of the things of which Bolingbroke accused him. However, if you do not turn

to Holinshed and Hall and the chroniclers, but turn
instead to Shakespeare, you will find that he deliberately
left the matter open, going counter to the sources that
were available to him, so that you cannot tell from his
play which was guilty. He leaves audiences in a state
of tension about the matter and doesn't say that Mowbray was guilty of the things that Bolingbroke charged
him with, even though he was.

I saw a performance of *Richard II* once in which, in
order to improve on Shakespeare, the director gathered
a scene from a play, called *Richard of Woodstock,* which
remained in manuscript until the twentieth century.
This scene showed the murder of the Duke of Gloucester
with Mowbray pounding about and saying, "Aha!"
nearby, thus removing all doubt of his guilt. I thought
this was deliberately going counter to the intentions of
the dramatist, who, although he knew himself that Mowbray was guilty, according to all of the history books
of the time, deliberately preferred to put the matter in
a state of tension and equilibrium so that he could leave
the audience in two minds about Mowbray's guilt. This
same point occurs again with regard to the guilt of
Aumerle in the same play, and I think to a certain
extent it exists with regard to the intervention of Wolsey
with the Earl of Buckingham in *Henry VIII*.

You are fortunate here in getting Shakespearean
productions that differ very much, and differ for the
better, from the kind of productions one sees in England
so much in the present day. There, the director says to
himself, "*Henry the Fifth,* well of course they saw Leslie
Banks three years ago; they saw Gielgud five years ago;
they saw Richardson seven years ago; they saw Irving

so many years ago. What can I do to be different from them? Shall they all ride bicycles, or shall they all come down (like bright exhalations) by parachute?" Their aim in directing a play is not to give proper interpretation of an existing set of words, but to give something which differs from the various productions which have gone before them.

Over here it is very much easier for you to see a Shakespeare play for the first time. In England, I have, without any kind of inconvenience, seen all the 37 plays of Shakespeare in the last twenty years, and very many of them half a dozen times. On one occasion, when I was somewhat crazy on the subject, I saw five different productions of *Richard II* in twelve months. If you are prepared to make use of British Railways, you can see an enormous amount of Shakespeare in the course of a year, and I think that here you are, to a certain extent, fortunate in being able to see plays for the first time.

I started seeing Shakespeare plays when I was about nine years old, and sometimes I find it very difficult to see the play as a play, I am so busy in saying, "Well! Of course Gielgud did that; and this is a great change from what Wolfit did." I find myself looking at directions and productions rather than allowing myself to be pleasured by the plays that are set before me.

I should like to spend hours and hours talking with lavish and fulsome praise about the plays which I have seen here in Stratford since I arrived. I have been seeing Shakespeare plays for forty-five years in England, in Germany, and the United States, and I am absolutely convinced that the best Shakespeare production I have ever seen was the *Love's Labour's Lost* I saw Monday.

There is one English stage director, whom I am not
going to name, but whose very evident purpose in the
direction of a Shakespeare play is to go very carefully
through the text and see wherever there is a line of full
poetic beauty. He puts a little mark in the margin, I'm
quite sure, and arranges for somebody to fire a gun or
turn a somersault. There was a production of *Romeo and
Juliet* by this man in which the stage was constantly
thick with tumblers turning somersaults. In another
production by this same person, he elected to have,
whenever there was a passage of poetic beauty, someone playing the drum.

I suppose it was a sort of theory that the English
public cannot take poetry or that English actors can't
deliver poetry. It is very similar to the performance you
get if you listen to some broadcast productions of Shakespeare. They work on the principle that no human
being can listen to more than ten consecutive lines of
poetry. If there is a thirty-line speech, after the tenth
line somebody says, "It that so?" or, "Well! Well! I am
surprised!" The whole speech is broken up into chew-
able snippets, which I don't find particularly necessary.

I've been talking in the most rambling way, tending
to an arrogant truculence, which I hope you will believe is affected. Some years ago I asked Professor Harbage, whom I delight to see here tonight, if he would
read through a piece I'd written about Shakespeare. He
very kindly read it through, making no charge, and
said, when he'd brought it back to me, "Do you want to
make enemies all over the world?" Looking as much like
Harpo Marx as I possibly could, I said with a gleeful

voice, "Yes." That of course is totally untrue. I wist-fully would say here that I am a humble person who wants to be loved, and not to be hated.

Let me also say, that it has been a frightening privi-lege to speak to you here; particularly when you have, before you listened to me, been listening to such people as Messrs. Harbage, Moore, Ferguson, and Langham. I feel very inadequate after them; and I don't remember who it was, but some poor literary hack some years ago wrote a sentence which I adopt in this connection; it runs as follows:

> "The words of Mercury are harsh after the songs of Apollo."

AFTERNOTE
This piece was composed for oral delivery and is there-fore different from what it would have been had I composed it as an article to be printed. I hope that if it contains anything good, I shall be given credit for it: if it contains what is bad, will the kind-hearted reader say "This failing would have been absent had he com-posed it as an article and not as an after-dinner speech"? The speech was tape-recorded and typed out and I have tinkered with it to some extent but, I am sure, not enough. Its manner is often (alas!) cheap and frivolous; but I have not deserted any of the opinions expressed in it.

59 Bonger sees thru th witch's flummery
60 Witches wish mach. well